A WINTERTHUR GUIDE TO
AMERICAN CHIPPENDALE FURNITURE

Middle Atlantic and Southern Colonies

WINTERTHUR

A WINTERTHUR GUIDE TO
AMERICAN CHIPPENDALE FURNITURE

Middle Atlantic and Southern Colonies

Charles F. Hummel

A Winterthur Book/Rutledge Books
Crown Publishers, Inc.

Abbreviations Used in Captions:

acc. no. = accession number
ca. = circa
cf. = compare
cm = centimeters
Diam = diameter
ed. = edition
H = height
L = length
W = width
w. = working

All the furniture illustrated in this book is from The Henry Francis du Pont Winterthur Museum. Except where noted, accession numbers preceded by the letter *G* indicate that the object illustrated was the gift of the late Henry Francis du Pont. Absence of a letter denotes a museum purchase. The primary wood is always listed first. Where secondary woods are omitted, either they were not originally present or they have been replaced.

Copyright © 1976 The Henry Francis du Pont Winterthur Museum. All rights reserved, including the right of reproduction in whole or in part.
Prepared and produced by Rutledge Books, a division of Arcata Consumer Products Corporation, 25 West 43 Street, New York, N.Y. 10036.
Published by Crown Publishers, Inc., One Park Avenue, New York, N.Y. 10016. Published simultaneously in Canada by General Publishing Company, Ltd.
First printing 1976
Printed in the United States of America

Library of Congress Cataloging in Publication Data
Hummel, Charles F
    A Winterthur guide to American Chippendale.

    "A Winterthur book/Rutledge."
    Bibliography: p. 144.
    1.   Furniture, Colonial—Middle Atlantic States.
2.   Furniture—Middle Atlantic States.   3.   Fur-
niture, Colonial—Southern States.   4.   Furniture
—Southern States.   5.   Decoration and ornament
—Chippendale style.   6.   Henry Francis du Pont
Winterthur Museum.   I.   Henry Francis du Pont
Winterthur Museum.   II.   Title.
NK2410.5.H85   1976   749.2′14   76-10845
ISBN 0-517-52176-8 paper
ISBN 0-517-52783-9 cloth

Contents

Introduction

In 1835, before the handcraft system of production in America had been replaced by modern industrial techniques, Alexis de Tocqueville characterized the utilitarian spirit in which Americans cultivated the arts: "They habitually put use before beauty, and they want beauty itself to be useful."[1] Almost seventy years earlier, the colonial American painter John Durand clearly recognized the indifference of his contemporaries to the fine arts. His pathetic advertisement in *The New York Journal* (April 7, 1768) noted that many of the public regarded painting as a "superfluous ornament." The genius of artistic expression in eighteenth-century America, therefore, was found in beautiful and useful objects produced for homes and public buildings. Among the highest forms of creative endeavor in the decorative arts was the furniture that was made by craftsmen working throughout the colonies. It was no accident that master craftsmen were often referred to as "artists in their trade." Whether a cabinetmaker, carver, or turner, their apprenticeship training included the development of skills necessary to produce drawings and sketches. This training also included knowledge of architectural design, especially the rules of the orders of architecture and considerable acquaintance with perspective and correct proportion. Thomas Chippendale, the English cabinetmaker whose name is associated with the style of furniture produced in America between 1755 and 1790, included instructive material on these subjects in all three editions of his design book, *The Gentleman & Cabinet-Maker's Director*. Indeed, he believed that the study of architecture and rules of perspective was "the very Soul and Basis" of the art of cabinetmaking.

Not all cabinetmakers in eighteenth-century America were artistic geniuses. Levels of competence varied, not only from region to region but within the same community. It was more difficult to hide incompetence in the production of furniture, where defects would be glaringly apparent to customers, than it was in a craft such as house carpentry.[2] It is hard for modern Americans to comprehend the degree of personal responsibility a master crafts-man in eighteenth-century society shouldered for the objects he produced. A cabinetmaker owned and operated a shop, purchased tools and raw materials, designed his products (often in consultation with his customers), supervised the work of journeymen, instructed apprentices, procured commissions for new work, and sold ready-made goods over the counter. Complaints, whether legitimate or not, were brought to the master cabinetmaker.

In part because of the personal nature of the craft, many apprentices and journeymen tried to remain within, or near, the community in which they had received their training. Their skill and integrity would be locally known, and such credentials were of great assistance in establishing a business in eighteenth-century America. They could also depend on the assistance of family, relatives, and friends in providing business contacts and possibly capital to help them set up as master cabinetmakers. Not every apprentice or journeyman could marry one of his master's daughters, although many did. That too, would tend to keep a craftsman close to the community in which he had been trained.

The cost in both time and money of moving goods overland was often prohibitive and contributed greatly to the maintenance of local traditions and customs, and also encouraged the use of locally grown woods for cabinetwork, especially in those parts of furniture not exposed to customers or admirers. Although the vast majority of surviving American and English furniture of this period is made from mahogany, it is clear that American cabinetmakers were also willing to produce the widest possible range of forms in walnut, cherry, maple, or pine. In 1755, the Philadelphia cabinet- and chairmaker Francis Trumble listed twenty-three different types of furniture that he could produce in any of the major woods just noted.[3] Lists of prices charged by cabinetmakers for furniture make it clear that the customer's taste and ability to pay determined the wood selected by cabinetmakers for furniture made in the Chippendale period.[4]

Mahogany was known to American cabinetmakers at least as early as 1708, when over thirty-six feet of "Mahogany Plank" were listed in the inventory of the Philadelphia shop of Charles Plumley. [5] Mahogany, a dense-grained hardwood with rich, lustrous patterns that could be enhanced by oil, wax, shellac, or varnish, was probably not fully appreciated until the introduction of the Chippendale style. Whatever the choice of major and secondary woods, colonial American cabinetmakers were more generous in their use of mahogany than were their English counterparts. The colonies were closer to the mahogany forests of the West Indies and Central America; consequently, cabinetmakers were not forced to treat it as so precious a commodity. Depending on the locale, forests close to every community provided quantities of white or yellow pine, red or white oak, maple, cherry, chestnut, red gum, ash, cypress, white cedar, tulipwood, and other woods used in the construction of furniture.

For all these reasons, American furniture in the Chippendale style tends to be a reflection of local construction habits and preferences for design generated by cabinetmakers and customers. New York cabinetmakers produced blocklike claw-and-ball feet, whereas Philadelphia artisans made theirs with prominent knuckles tightly grasping a flattened ball. Finials on Massachusetts case pieces are usually shaped like a corkscrew; their counterparts in Philadelphia simulate flames. Why did New York artisans prefer to taper the rear legs of their chairs and finish them with a rectangular pad? Why did Philadelphia woodworkers prefer to use a "stump" rear leg, merely rounding the edges of their stock? Records provide no clues for these regional preferences, yet study of collections of American furniture show that they existed.

This guide is arranged to encourage the comparison of forms produced within a given region with those made in other centers. Value judgments about construction, skill, proportion, the success of ornamentation—a kind of internal and external "good, better, and best"—should result for the reader. [6]

Initially, it is more important to develop a comparative sense of quality in furniture than it is to become familiar with craftsmen's labels, ownership by persons of historical importance, family histories, or other means of "documentation" for furniture.

Very few pieces of American furniture bear the brand, label, or stamp of their makers. Labels, histories, original accounts or bills, or other documentation add to the price of antique furniture, but they add nothing to its aesthetic merit. Documentation helps to establish the existence of a form at a given time and in a given place, all of which is helpful because it advances knowledge and provides standards for comparison. Only by training the eye to see visual details—and then remembering them—can an individual begin to identify furniture of excellent quality.

It was part of the genius of Henry Francis du Pont that he assembled examples of furniture representative of the highest quality of typical forms produced by American cabinetmakers. He was not interested in unique forms because one could not learn enough from them. The Winterthur collection of American Chippendale furniture numbers more then 625 examples, and that figure does not include small forms (such as boxes), Windsor furniture, or furniture produced by non-English cultural groups such as the Pennsylvania Germans.

It is not surprising, in view of the museum's geographical location, that the collection's greatest strength lies in Chippendale furniture made in the Middle Atlantic colonies. The collection of New England Chippendale furniture would be considered superb by almost any other museum. Like most museums, Winterthur lacks comparable collections of Southern furniture. During the period from 1926 to 1961, when most of the collection was assembled, Southern furniture was neither readily available to Northern collectors, nor had much of it been clearly identified. Excellent collections of Southern furniture are available to the public at Colonial Williamsburg and the Museum of Early Southern Decorative Arts in Winston-Salem, North Carolina. The 151 pieces of furniture illustrated in this guide are a careful sampling of furniture at Winterthur made between 1755 and 1790 in New York, Philadelphia, and the South and, with the exception of the latter, are indicative of the range of forms produced in those areas.

The construction techniques and design of American Chippendale were derived from English, Irish, and Scottish sources.

Richard Magrath, in Charleston, South Carolina, advertised in 1772 that he was making "carved Chairs of the newest fashion . . . of the same Pattern as those imported by Peter Manigault, Esq." [7] Some colonial Americans became acquainted with the new style in the course of their travels overseas. Emigrant cabinetmakers from the British Isles were another important factor in transmitting style and techniques. John Brinner, a cabinet- and chairmaker in New York City, advertised in 1762 that he was "from London," noting that he had "brought over from London six artificers well skill'd in the above Branches." [8] Any one of these varied sources could account for such specific relationships as, for example, the similarity between the five-legged card and gaming tables made in New York (Figures 31 and 32) and a similar English table in the collection of Temple Newsam, Leeds, England. [9] Government officials traveled from the British Isles to the colonies, and it can be assumed that they carried with them their fashion-conscious tastes. The influence of English design on colonial America in this period is best summarized by a sentence contained in a letter of May 18, 1765, from Captain Samuel Morris of Philadelphia to his nephew Samuel Powel, Jr., residing in London. "Household goods may be had here as cheap and as well made from English patterns." [10]

Cabinetmakers were accustomed to making furniture with the aid of paper or wood patterns. A Chippendale side chair, for example, might require separate patterns for the crest rail, splat, seat rails, front legs, and one large, continuous pattern for a rear leg and stile. A cabinetmaker's stock of patterns was as important as his awls, chisels, marking gauges, planes, and saws. Unlike most hand tools, however, patterns became stylistically obsolete and few eighteenth- or early nineteenth-century examples survive.

For some years prior to the introduction of the Chippendale style into colonial America, English craftsmen and designers had published books of designs for architecture and ornamental furniture from which patterns could be copied or modified. [11] None, however, had an impact in the English-speaking world comparable to *The Gentleman & Cabinet-Maker's Director*, published in 1754 by one of the foremost of the London cabinetmakers, Thomas Chippendale (ca. 1718–1779). Although it was a summary of current English fashion, the original contribution of his book, resulting in its widespread acceptance, was the fact that for the first time, it contained "Elegant and Useful Designs of Household Furniture In the Most Fashionable Taste." In addition to ornamental luxuries for aristocratic or wealthy patrons, the *Director* contained designs "suited to the Fancy and Circumstances of Persons in all Degrees of Life." [12] Subsequent editions published in 1755 and 1762 attest to its popularity.

A copy of the 1762 edition of Chippendale's *Director* was owned by the Library Company of Philadelphia shortly after its publication. Many of that city's cabinetmakers were members of the library and would have had access to the design book. [13] Thomas Affleck, a Philadelphia cabinetmaker, is said to have owned a personal copy of the *Director*. [14] In 1776, Robert Bell published in Philadelphia *American Independence the Interest and Glory of Great Britain*. Inside the back board is Bell's advertisement for new and used books of which No. 29 is "Chippendale's 160 elegant and useful designs of household furniture." Because the third edition of 1762 contains 200 plates, it is obvious that the 1754 or 1755 edition was in Robert Bell's stock. Thus the complete range of designs published by Thomas Chippendale was available to Philadelphia's woodworkers. Among the stock of books that James Rivington, a bookseller, brought with him from London in 1760 was the recently published *Household Furniture in Genteel Taste*. It contained designs by leading craftsmen of London, including Thomas Chippendale. Rivington offered it for sale in New York and Philadelphia shops. [15] It is certain that English architectural and furniture design books were available to many skilled craftsmen from Boston to Charleston, South Carolina, during the Chippendale period.

Colonial newspaper advertisements make clear that from whatever source—imported furniture, emigrant craftsmen, visual ideas carried in the eyes and minds of travelers, or design books—it did not take long for the new style to be introduced to the American colonies. In 1755, only a year after the publication of Chippendale's *Director*, a public vendue in Boston offered for sale "an exceeding good sett of Mahogany carv'd Chairs, new Fashion." In the same year, Francis Trumble of Philadelphia listed ready-made furniture "after the newest fashions." [16]

What were the major design components of the "newest fashion" in English and American furniture? Chippendale described them in 1754 as being in the "Gothic, Chinese and modern taste," which by 1762 was crystallized on the title page of the *Director* in the phrase "the most fashionable taste." During the second quarter of the eighteenth century, admiration for the ruins of Gothic structures became a mark of sophistication, and a strong interest in Gothic architecture inspired a revival of interest in Gothic furniture. Chippendale and other designers did not, of course, advocate copying the furniture of the Middle Ages. In keeping with the spirit of this new ornamental style, he showed furniture designs incorporating cusps, pointed arcades, tracery, quatrefoils, and other late-medieval motifs. Colonial Americans used similar ornament on their furniture, as can be seen in Figures 7, 11, 36, 44, and 53−57. Chinese and Japanese decorative art began to exert a strong influence on European art after trade with the Far East expanded in the seventeenth century. Chinese influence in furniture design of this period can be discerned in the use of fretwork, railing, lattice, and straight-legged chairs and tables. The Chinese taste also had its American translation (Figures 9, 19, 33, 81, 85, and 90).

To Thomas Chippendale and his colonial American contemporaries, "modern taste" was a phrase used to describe the exciting ornamental style that abandoned the rigid, structural concepts of classical design and adopted curvilinear, asymmetrical arrangements of pierced shells, foliage, flowers, dripping vegetation, and other natural forms. Originating in France during the last quarter of the seventeenth century and undergoing continuous refinement in that country until the 1760s, it was referred to by artists, craftsmen, and designers as *le gout moderne*, translated precisely as "the modern taste." This unbalanced, sometimes exaggerated, decorative vocabulary is often identified by the term *rococo*, but not until the early nineteenth century was that term used, and then only in a pejorative sense. [17] The term *Chippendale* was not used as an adjective to describe a furniture style until 1876 when it appeared in the English novel *An Odd Couple* by Mrs. Oliphant. An American edition appeared three years later in New York City.

Because the "modern taste" evolved gradually and never made a complete break with the classical tradition, it was widely accepted in England and colonial America. This style could embrace a traditional English Gothic strain, incorporate exotic elements from China, use classical ornament, and still satisfy the dictates of the English painter William Hogarth. In his *Analysis of Beauty* (1753), Hogarth had defined the S-curve, or cyma-recta, as the ultimate "line of beauty." Although he made his specific illustration a curved leg of a chair, the cabriole leg introduced early in the eighteenth century, he made it clear that this serpentine line should dominate the shape of furniture. "How inelegant would be the shape of all our moveables without it." [18] The designs in Thomas Chippendale's *Director* provided illustrations for all these style elements, helping to popularize them and eventually creating an image that made his name synonymous with the style.

Undoubtedly helping to popularize this style was the fact that few truly new furniture forms were introduced in England or America during the Chippendale period. On these shores, a number of small furniture forms for specialized purposes, evidence of increasing wealth and a taste for luxury, were developed. Fire screens to protect people from hot coals popping from a fireplace were a useful and attractive innovation (Figures 20–21 and 88–89). A profusion of stands to support basins, candlesticks, and kettles came into existence (Figures 25–29, 95, and 133–134). In New England and Charleston, South Carolina, the breakfront bookcase made its appearance. Never a common form, probably because of its expense, this type of furniture was called a library bookcase by Chippendale. Kneehole bureau tables (Figure 109), sometimes used as desks but more frequently for dressing and grooming, had been known in Boston in small quantities between 1739 and 1752. Their popularity grew during the Chippendale period. China tables (Figures 36 and 135), with Gothic or Chinese pierced galleries, were a variant of the long-known tea table. New Pembroke, or breakfast, tables (Figures 96—97) with narrow leaves and broad tops offered a practical contrast to earlier drop-leaf examples constructed with narrow tops and wide leaves.

American cabinetmakers continued to make the high chest of drawers and developed it to the highest possible expression of a furniture form (Figures 81—83 and Plate XI). It provided ample storage for clothing and linens, but in England it was abandoned in favor of the clothes press and the double chest of drawers.

Despite the lack of new forms introduced in this period, American craftsmen introduced novelty in their furniture in a variety of ways. Perhaps the most striking change was the transformation of the solid splats of Queen Anne style arm- and side chairs into light, airy, fragile, but serviceable, backrests. Instead of using hoop-back or yoke-back crest rails that curved into the rear stiles, chairmakers now shaped the top or crest rail like a bow and supported it on the rear stiles. The results can be disturbing because the vertical thrust of the stiles is cut off abruptly. The unbalanced, asymmetrical effect was enhanced when the ends of crest rails were carved with elaborate shells or cabochon—a convex, peanut-shaped decoration (Figures 45 and 56).

In a nod to Chinese influence, straight legs were used for beds, chairs, sofas, and tables. These could be plain, carved or molded, and some terminated in blocks called Marlborough feet (Figures 48—49 and 85). Strong evidence of the continuity of earlier forms into the Chippendale period is the persistence of the claw-and-ball foot in American furniture. This type of foot was old-fashioned, not in the "modern taste," and none is illustrated in the *Director*. On the other hand, it did have a strong relationship to the natural ornament so prevalent in the new style. Carved hairy-paw or scroll feet were types occasionally employed by colonial artisans (Figures 50—52). They were quite stylish and are illustrated in Chippendale's design book.

The serpentine line, or S-curve, so admired by William Hogarth and his contemporaries, was incorporated into the production of American case furniture or tables in a number of ingenious ways. Tops, drawer fronts, and skirts of card tables and chests of drawers might be serpentine (Figures 17, 31−32, 78, and 105). Ogee-bracket feet supported desks, desk and bookcases, chests of drawers, double chests, and tall-case clocks (Figures 86−87, 126, and 132). Repetition of cyma-curves on the edges of tilt-top tea tables produced the piecrust edge sought after by modern collectors (Figures 34, and 115−117).

By now it should be obvious that the nature of the rococo style is ornament, not structure. Most cabinetmakers simply grafted the new style of decoration onto established furniture forms. It is possible that American cabinetmakers quickly and readily accepted the new style because it was not necessary to retool. Existing patterns could be used to produce basic furniture shapes and the decoration of surfaces turned over to another woodworking specialist, the carver. Most cabinetmakers were not skilled in manipulating the chisels and gouges used by woodcarvers. The more exuberant, naturalistic forms that we associate with rococo taste were beyond their abilities. It is no accident that the most successful examples of American Chippendale furniture were produced in Philadelphia and Boston, where several carvers could be supported by a large number of cabinetmakers. Furniture carving in New York tends to be less successful, although at its best it competes with that of Philadelphia (Figure 37).

No matter how high the quality of ornament added to American furniture, the overall result would not have been successful had the basic forms been badly designed. Readers will find many authorities who claim for American furniture "an elegant simplicity" of design. Perhaps! In fact, however, the appearance of all furniture produced in America and England in this style was more likely to be related to the wealth and taste of the customer. Set prices were charged for every variation from a basic form. The amount of carving, molded edges, brackets, and so forth was dependent to a large degree on ability to pay for these "extras." An eighteenth-century gentleman ordering furniture faced the same problem as the twentieth-century car buyer confronted with myriad "options." Among the most popular English architectural design books in the American colonies were Abraham Swan's *The British Architect* (London, 1745) and *A Collection of Designs in Architecture* (London, 1757). The preface to both the American and English versions of the latter contains advice to artisans to make the original design as good as possible and not to overload any design with ornament.

American artisans and their customers could not ignore the influence of classical restraint that was part of their English cultural heritage and, therefore, they used the ornament provided by the Chippendale style with taste and good judgment. Exciting decoration grafted onto traditional, pleasing forms was a formula for successful design that has delighted owners of American Chippendale furniture ever since the eighteenth century.

Notes

1. Alexis de Tocqueville, *Democracy in America*, ed. J. P. Mayer and Max Lerner, new translation by George Lawrence (New York: Harper & Row, 1966), p. 432.
2. Peter C. Marzio, "Carpentry in the Southern Colonies during the Eighteenth Century with Emphasis on Maryland and Virginia," *Winterthur Portfolio 7* (Charlottesville: The University Press of Virginia, 1972), pp. 229–250.
3. *Pennsylvania Gazette* (Philadelphia), Jan. 14. 1755.
4. Harrold E. Gillingham, "Benjamin Lehman, A Germantown Cabinetmaker," *The Pennsylvania Magazine of History and Biography*, 54 (1930), pp. 289–306. Charles F. Montgomery, *American Furniture: The Federal Period* (New York: The Viking Press, 1966), p. 20.
5. William Macpherson Hornor, Jr., *Blue Book. Philadelphia Furniture* (Philadelphia: Privately printed, 1935), p. 9.
6. The visual approach was pioneered by Albert Sack, *Fine Points of Furniture: Early American* (New York: Crown Publishers, 1950).
7. *South Carolina Gazette* (Charleston), July 9, 1772.
8. *New York Mercury*, May 31, 1762.
9. Morrison H. Heckscher, "The New York Serpentine Card Table," *Antiques*, (May 1973), pp. 954–963.
10. Quoted in Hornor. *Blue Book*, p. 81.
11. Peter Ward-Jackson, *English Furniture Designs of the Eighteenth Century* (London: Victoria and Albert Museum, 1958), pp. 1–21.
12. Thomas Chippendale, *The Gentleman & Cabinet-Maker's Director* (1762; reprint ed., New York: Dover Publications, Inc., 1966), title page.
13. Charles F. Hummel, "The Influence of English Design Books Upon the Philadelphia Cabinetmaker, 1760–1780" (M.A. thesis, University of Delaware, 1955), pp. 50–53.
14. Hornor, *Blue Book*, pp. 73, 78.
15. Hummel, "The Influence of English Design Books," pp. 53–54. Ward-Jackson, *English Furniture Designs*, pp. 51–52.
16. *Boston Gazette*, Nov. 17, 1755. *Pennsylvania Gazette*, Jan. 14, 1755.
17. Sidney Fiske Kimball, *The Creation of the Rococo* (Philadelphia: Philadelphia Museum of Art, 1943), pp. 3–6, 223–225.
18. As quoted in Ward-Jackson, *English Furniture Designs*, p. 9.

New York

Figure 1   Figure 2

Figures 1 and 2. *Armchairs. These armchairs typify
the ample proportions associated with New York
seating furniture, differing only slightly from
Philadelphia examples in their overall size (Figs.
39-47). New York chairmakers created an illusion of
wide, heavy furniture. The outward thrust of arm
supports, armrests, and seat rails, combined with
broad splats make the chairs seem larger than chairs
made elsewhere. The chairs appear to be identical,
but a closer look reveals differences in the carving
of the armrest terminals, splats, and crest rails.
Figure 2 is also slightly smaller and has no molded
edge on its shoe, or splat, rail. Armchairs and side
chairs similar to these were made for many New York
families, which should warn that it is possible to
assemble a "set" of chairs. Fig. 1: mahogany;
1765-75; H 39¼" (99.6 cm); no. IX of a set; acc. no.
G59.2826. Fig. 2: mahogany; 1765-75; H 38¹⁵⁄₁₆"
(98.8 cm); acc. no. G59.2827.*

Figure 3

Figures 3 and 4. *Corner Chairs.* Roundabouts *were chairs that could fit under the writing lid of a desk, hold a commode (Fig. 3), or be placed in a corner. These chairs exemplify the restrained New York interpretation of the Chippendale style. In Figure 4, heart-and-diamond-shaped cutouts in the otherwise solid, Queen Anne-style splat, and leaf-carving on the front leg concede to the new style. Square-sectioned claw-and-ball feet (Fig. 4) are common on New York furniture of this period. Figure 3 has feet closer to those found on Philadelphia furniture. Fig. 3: mahogany, red gum; 1760-75; H 32" (81.3 cm); acc. no. G60.779. Fig. 4: mahogany, cherry; 1750-60; H 32" (81.3 cm); acc. no. G59.2838.*

Figure 4

Figure 5

Figures 5 and 6. *Side Chairs. The splat design of these chairs (interlaced elements centering on a diamond motif) was frequently used in New York, but variations of it occur on chairs from other regions. Handsome but rigidly controlled and shallow carving is a distinctive New York feature (Fig. 5a). The rear feet of Figure 5 (Fig. 5c) and the four-square claw-and-ball feet of Figure 6 are also familiar New York features. But the front feet of Figure 5 and the so-called stump rear legs of Figure 6 are more characteristic of Philadelphia chairs. An unoriginal inscription (Fig. 6a) has been the basis for attributing much New York furniture to Gilbert Ash.[1] Fig. 5: mahogany, red cedar, red oak, white pine; 1755-65; H 39⅛" (99.3 cm); one of a pair; acc. no. G57.545.1. Fig. 6: mahogany, American beech; 1755-65; H 38¾" (98.4 cm); no. III of a set; acc. no. G56.98.3.*

Figure 5a

Figure 5b

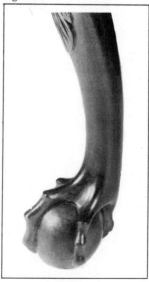

Figure 5c

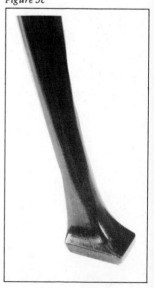

Figure 6

Figure 7

Figures 7 and 8. *Side Chairs. The shaped rear leg ending in a platform, found on so many New York chairs (Figs. 5c, 7), is derived from English sources. Seating a splat directly into a combined rear seat rail and shoe (Fig. 7) is also an English practice. In colonial America, splats were usually seated in a separate shoe attached to the rear seat rail (Fig. 8). Figure 7 includes stop-fluted stiles, Gothic arches and tracery, and ruffle carving on the splat. The crest rail is related to Figure 8, but in recognition of the "modern" taste it turns up to form slight ears. With a balloon seat, shell carving on the crest rail and knees, and a crest rail flowing into its stiles Figure 8 is an illustration of Queen Anne design retained well into the Chippendale period. According to family tradition, it is one of a set of 12 chairs made about 1779 when General Samuel Blachley Webb married Elizabeth Bancker. Fig. 7: mahogany, soft maple, birch; 1760-80; H 37⅞″ (96.2 cm); acc. no. G52.243. Fig. 8: mahogany, red gum, oak, tulip; 1770-80; H 39¼″ (99.6 cm); no. II of a set; acc. no. G59.2835.*

Figure 8

Figure 9 Figure 10

Figures 9 and 10. *Side Chairs. A serpentine crest rail, pronounced ears with leaf carving, foliage carving—once described as "dripping stalactites"—on the splat, pierced and unpierced fretwork on the stretchers, and straight front legs indicate that the maker and owner of Figure 9 were conversant with the Chippendale style. Robert Manwaring's* The Cabinet and Chair Maker's Real Friend and Companion *(London, 1765) contains a design from which the splat of Figure 10 was adapted. Punchwork accents a portion of the splats of both chairs. Square claw-and-ball feet and a feeling of solid expanse, heightened by carved gadrooning on the front seat rail, are aspects of New York origin. Fig. 9: mahogany, white oak; 1760-80; H 39¼″ (99.6 cm); acc. no. 57.51. Fig. 10: mahogany; 1765-75; H 38⅝″ (98.1 cm); no. VII of a set, one of a pair; acc. no. G52.244.1.*

Figure 11

Figures 11 and 12. *Side Chairs. Figure 11 is proof that sophisticated chairs were produced in New York City. Plate XIII (1754 ed.) and Plate X (1762 ed.) of Chippendale's* Director *furnished the design source for its back. Typically, elements such as the pierced crest rail and Gothic arches in the splat were selected and rearranged. Chippendale's advice for chairs of this type was followed by many American craftsmen: "If you think they are too much ornamented, that can be omitted at pleasure." Somewhat freer rococo carving on the knee brackets of Figure 12 and the simple device of dividing the crest rail as it joins the splat to produce a* ribband *effect, make this tassel-back chair appear superior to chairs that are related to Figures 1 and 2. These chairs were owned originally by the Wright family of Oyster Bay, N.Y. (Fig. 11) and by Elias Boudinot, lawyer, patriot, and statesman whose family was rooted in New York and New Jersey (Fig. 12). Fig. 11: mahogany; 1765–80; H 38½" (97.8 cm); no. VIII in a set, one of four; acc. no. G58.1784.4. Fig. 12: mahogany, red pine; 1765–80. H 38½" (97.8 cm); acc. no. G51.66.2.*

Figure 12

Figure 13

Figures 13 and 14. *Back and Foot Stools. Side chairs with upholstered seats and backs (Fig. 13) were called French, stool back, back stool, and stuffed chairs in the Chippendale period. Newspapers record their use in New York by 1765 and Rita Susswein Gottesman's* The Arts and Crafts in New York, 1726-1776 *records that Theodosius Fowler, upholsterer, advertised in 1774 that he made "backstool chairs finished in the genteelest and newest taste." Upholstery was expensive in the 18th century and, therefore, many colonial chairs only have upholstered slip seats. It is only a "best guess" that these stools were made in New York. Both have cherry seat frames, a wood used by cabinetmakers there but also employed elsewhere for construction. The similarity of the "Chinese Chippendale" molded straight legs and plain stretchers of both stools is obvious. The legs of a New York slab, or pier, table may also be related to these stools (Fig. 33). Other upholstered New York furniture is illustrated in Plates I through III. Fig. 13: mahogany, cherry; 1765-80; H 37¼" (94.5 cm); acc. no. G59.1876. Fig. 14: mahogany, cherry, white pine; 1765-85; H 18½" (47 cm); acc. no. G59.2845.*

Figure 14

Figure 15

Figures 15, 16, and 17.
Chests of Drawers. For case furniture, cabinet-makers determined their price partially on the number of drawers to be fashioned. It follows that the most popular storage form of the period was the chest of drawers. Thick, square feet, and deeply notched, cyma-curved "swelled brackets" virtually identical, characterize Figures 15 and 16. The top drawer of Figure 15 is fitted with compartments to hold necessities for the toilet of an 18th-century gentleman. "Dressing chests" were advertised for sale in New York City in 1773. It seems an appropriate name for this form. Of three similar examples, two bear the label of Samuel Prince, who kept a cabinet shop at the "Sign of the Chest of Drawers" in New York City.² Figure 17 reveals (all at extra cost) stop fluting (see Pl. I; Fig. 7), leaf-and-dart carving on the ogee-shaped edge of its top, leaf carving on its bracket feet, a writing slide, and serpentine front. It is not surprising, then, to find the Van Rensselaer name inscribed back of the writing slide. Fig. 15: mahogany, tulip; 1770-80; H 32¼" (81.9 cm); acc. no. G52.143. Fig. 16: mahogany, tulip; 1765-80; H 33¼" (84.4 cm); acc. no. G58.1787. Fig. 17: mahogany, tulip; 1765-80; H 33" (83.8 cm); acc. no. G54.86.

Figure 16

Figure 17

Figure 18. *Desk. New York cabinetmakers preferred straight, unadorned lines for desks as well as chests of drawers. Carved gadrooning often relieved the horizontal thrust of their plain fronts. Many New York desks were made with claw-and-ball feet at the front, and heavy, ogee-bracket feet supporting the rear corners—a characteristic shared with Rhode Island and Connecticut furniture. Plain desks probably cost three to four times as much as chests of drawers. The investment was considered practical by many people because a desk provided storage, a degree of security for valuable papers, and surfaces to be used to carry on correspondence. Fig. 18: mahogany, tulip; 1765-80; H 45" (114.2 cm); acc. no. G58.1786.*

Figure 18

Figure 19

Figure 19. *Desk and Book-case. Thomas Chippendale and his contemporaries referred to this form as a* desk and bookcase. *It was one of the most expensive case pieces available in the 18th century. Few were made with glazed doors in the colonies. Cornice, central door, and pigeonholes of the desk section, and brasses all reflect a blind or pierced fret in a diamond and saltire design. Its "swelled" bracket feet are decorated with C-scrolls and acanthus-leaf carving. A design for a pediment bookcase in* Household Furniture in Genteel Taste for the Year 1760 *served as its source. On the basis of a similar desk and bookcase bearing Samuel Prince's label, Figure 19 is attributed to his shop. Fig. 19: mahogany, tulip, white pine; 1770-75; H 98½" (250.2 cm); acc. no. G51.31.*

29

Figure 20　　　　　*Figure 21*

Figures 20 and 21. *Fire Screens. Without such evidence as the panel on Figure 20 (by Tanneke Pears "IN NEW YORK YEAR 1766") it is difficult to relate fire screens to a school of cabinetmaking. But some clues are usually present. An urn and Tuscan or Doric columnar shaft (Fig. 20) relate to two New York candlestands (Figs. 26, 27), a tea table, and a New York fire screen.[3] The baluster shaft and shallow New York-type carving on the knees of Figure 21 are identical to those on a New York tripod-base tea table at the Albany Institute. (See also Fig. 25; Pl. IV). Fig. 20: mahogany; dated 1766; H 59⅝″ (151.4 cm); acc. no. G65.2903. Fig. 21: mahogany; 1760-75; H 61¼″ (155.6 cm); acc. no. G58.1788.*

Figure 22

Figure 22. *Looking Glass. Figure 22 is a fine example of one type of looking glass known to have been used in New York. During the Chippendale period, New Yorkers were told that they could purchase looking glasses imported from London in frames or that frames "in the most elegant and newest fashion" could be carved for them in their city. At present it is thought that the basic mahogany veneer on spruce frame is English and the carved white pine and tulip gilt ornaments were added in New York. The C-scroll and leaf carving applied to its crest; and pendant fruit, leaves, and flowers at its sides, signified recognition of the "modern taste." Fig. 22: mahogany veneer on spruce, white pine, tulip; 1775-90; H 51¾" (131.4 cm); acc. no. G59.795.*

Figure 23

frame. Figure 24 was originally in the Imlay House, Allentown, N.J. Its construction of walnut veneer over spruce and Scots pine carvings indicate that it was imported from England. Fig. 23: mahogany veneer over spruce, white pine; 1755-90; H 61¼" (155.6 cm); acc. no. G58.2142. Fig. 24: walnut veneer over spruce, Scots pine; 1755-90; H 69" (175.2 cm); one of a pair; acc. no. G57.664.1.

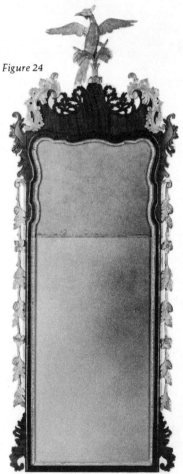

Figure 24

Figures 23 and 24. *Looking Glasses.* A simpler version of Figure 23, in the Albany Institute of History and Art, bears the stamp of its owner, Philip Van Rensselaer. In 1794, Winterthur's example was presented by Martha Washington to the wife of John E. Van Alen, congressman from Rensselaer County, N.Y. It has a white pine backboard and carved phoenix with mahogany veneer over an English spruce

Plate I

Plate I. *Bed. In colonial America, the term
bedstead meant the frame, headboard, and posts. Bed
furniture referred to matched hangings, as in this
set of English indigo resist-dyed cotton. The bed
has typical New York cabriole legs with leaf-carved
knees and square claw-and-ball feet. Other New York
examples have stop fluting (Figs. 7, 17). The rear
posts, usually plain and covered by a side curtain,
are here tapered and end in turned balusters supported
by pedestal bases. Pl. I: mahogany; 1760-75; H 87″
(221 cm); acc. no. G55.799.*

Plate II. *Easy Chair. The blue upholstery (1750-70) of this New York chair is appropriate because New York newspapers indicate that English silk damasks were sold there by upholsterers. However, the fabric would usually have been wool worsted damask or printed cotton. New York upholsterers used brass-headed nails to finish furniture. In 1762, lightning, coming down the chimney of a house, ran along "the Brass Nails that was in a Settee near the Hearth, blackening the Heads of all of them."[4] Massive looking, only the leaf-carved knees of this chair reflect the "modern taste." Pl. II: mahogany; 1760-75; H 46" (116.8 cm); acc. no. G57.533.*

Plate II

Plate III

Plate III. *Sofa. John Brinner, a New York cabinet- and chairmaker from London, indicated in 1762 that he made sofa, couch, and easy chair frames. John Brewer, an upholsterer in the same city, stuffed and covered the same forms.[5] A plain Marlborough-legged sofa frame, with plain stretchers, cost little more than a walnut chest of drawers, but "Stuffing and covering" added considerably to its expense. A New York serpentine back sofa with similar scrolled arms and rectangular stretchers is owned by the Henry Ford Museum. Some Rhode Island sofas of this period are similar, but microanalysis of its structure, covered in French green and white silk lampas (ca. 1750), indicates that it was made in New York. Pl. III: mahogany, American beech, red gum, yellow pine; 1770-80; L 105¾" (268.6 cm); acc. no. G51.6.*

Plate IV

closely related to Figure
34, but in neither example
is the carving in the high
relief that is associated
with tilt-top tables made
in Philadelphia (Figs. 115-
18). According to Joseph
Downs, this table was found
in Albany. In the
advertisement of the sale
of household furniture noted
above, "A Sett of fine Tea
Table China" was also to be
sold, indicating clearly the
purpose of these handsome
tables.[6] Pl. IV: mahogany,
cherry; 1765-75; H 28¼"
(71.7 cm), Diam 31⅞"
(81.6 cm); acc. no. G59.2928.

Plate IV. Tea Table. "A
round Mahogany Pillar, and
Claw Table" offered for
sale in New York City in
1763 is a succinct
description that might
apply to Plate IV. If the
term scallopt (scalloped)
had been added for the
piecrust edge of this tea
table, no doubt would exist
about its application. Leaf
carving on the knee and
vase-shaped baluster, a
fluted pillar or column,
and typical New York
tripod-base claw feet,
leave little doubt of the
table's origin. It is

Figure 25

Figure 25a

Figure 25. *Tilt-Top Candlestand. Candlestands
were the result of wood turning and joinery.
Whether city cabinetmakers always purchased parts
from turners for assembly on tripod bases or
sometimes turned and shaped all the necessary parts,
as did country craftsmen like Nathaniel Dominy V of
East Hampton, N.Y., is not known. Less expensive
than tables, they held not only candlesticks but a
variety of ceramic and metal objects. In this
period, the piecrust edge so highly prized today
(Fig. 25a) was referred to as scallopt. The feet
and legs of this stand are closely related to a
tripod-base tea table made for Robert Sanders of
Albany.[7] Fig. 25: mahogany: 1760-80; H 28" (71.7 cm);
Diam 24" (61 cm); acc. no. G65.2904.*

Figures 26 and 27.
Candlestands. Shallow knee carving—here in the form of fleur-de-lis, V-shaped lambrequin, and acanthus leaf—combined with a turned urn and Doric or Tuscan columnar shaft relate Figure 26 to other New York screens, stands, and tables. A heavy disc separating an urn or baluster shape from the base of the shaft is frequently seen on New York stands. The platform and squat posts supporting the top of Figure 27, called a birdcage, *permitted it to revolve as well as tilt up and down. It was used in any locale where a customer would pay the extra cost required by adding this feature to a stand. New York tripod-base furniture of this period might have claw-and-ball, paw, and carved or plain dolphin feet (Figs. 25-27). The carved C-scrolls circling its top (Fig. 27) contrast with the plain, dished top of Figure 26. Leaf carving and fluting on baluster- or vase-shaped shafts occur on other New York tables (Pl. IV; Fig. 34). Fig. 26: mahogany; 1760-75; H 26⅝" (67.6 cm), Diam 20½" (52.1 cm); acc. no. G64.663. Fig. 27: mahogany; 1760-75; H 28½" (72.4 cm), Diam 21¾" (55.2 cm); acc. no. G58.1778.*

Figure 26

Figure 27

Figures 28 and 29. *Basin, or
Washstands. Figure 28 was once
thought to be of Massachusetts origin,*[8]
*but its tulip drawer linings—a wood
not used in Massachusetts furniture of
this period—shallow C-scroll and
acanthus-leaf carving on its knees,
claw-and-ball feet, and Doric columns
supporting a shelf of drawers are
attributes of other New York furniture.*

Figure 29

Figure 28

*Except for its secondary woods, Figure
29 provides few clues to its origin.
Doric or Tuscan columns support a top
shelf and the drawer is fashioned of
red gum, a wood frequently used for
hidden furniture construction by New
York cabinetmakers. Fig. 28:
mahogany, tulip; 1770-80; H 31⅝"
(80.3 cm); acc. no. G58.2269. Fig.
29: mahogany, red gum; 1780-95; H 31¼"
(79.4 cm); acc. no. G61.139.*

Figure 30

Figure 30. *Gaming Table. Card and gaming tables, often made in pairs, supplied playing surfaces for dicing, backgammon,˙chess, and many card games. As with other gaming tables, this one has a baize-covered top, pockets for coins or counters, and insets for candlesticks. Five legs; gadroon-carved skirt; square or blocklike claw-and-ball feet; asymmetrical C-scroll, leaf, ruffle, and punchwork carving on the front knees (Fig. 30a) are all features this table shares with related examples (cf. n. 9). Its straight frame, circular candlestick insets, and smaller size are unusual (Figs. 31, 32). Fig. 30: mahogany, red gum, white oak, white pine, tulip; 1765-80; H (open) 27″ (68.6 cm); acc. no. G51.73.*

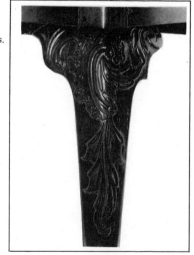

Figure 30a

Figure 31

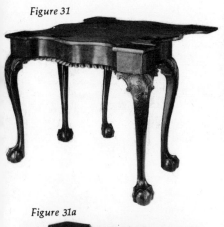

Figure 31a

Figures 31 and 32. *Gaming Tables. Five-legged card, or gaming, tables with bold, sinuous, serpentine-curved frames; gadrooned-carved front skirts; square corner insets for candlesticks; C-scroll, leaf, and ruffle carving on their knees; and sturdy claw-and-ball feet were the most successful furniture form made by New York cabinetmakers in the Chippendale period. A secret drawer, concealed behind the flying rail of the swing leg (Fig. 31a), was customary on New York tables of this type. Occasionally, the practice was also followed in Philadelphia (Fig. 99). Unlike Figure 30, these tables have partial carving decorating their rear knee brackets or knees. Stylistic and technical differences in carving on knees and skirt are obvious when these tables are compared. Figure 31 is described by Morrison Heckscher as a Van Rensselaer type, and Figure 32 is closely related to a Beekman family table owned by The New-York Historical Society.[9] Fig. 31: mahogany, American beech, cherry, black gum, white pine; 1760-75; H 29¼" (74.3 cm); acc. no. G59.2843. Fig. 32: mahogany, white pine, tulip; 1770-80; H 27½" (69.7 cm); acc. no. G58.1791.*

Figure 32

Figure 33

Figure 33. *Side Table. The clean, simple
lines of Chinese furniture design dovetailed
with the classical taste that remained
strong throughout this period. Figure 33 is
a New York cabinetmaker's version of a
"Sideboard Table" that appeared in all three
editions of the* Director *(Pl. LVI, 1762
ed.). Its heavy legs, softened by
molding, were needed to support the weight
of a marble top. The* New York Mercury
*(Dec. 28, 1767) offered "choice Marble
Slabs, for Side-Tables." In 1760, Mrs.
James Alexander of New York City bequeathed
to her daughter, "the marble tables that
now are in the Dining Room."*[10] *Fig. 33:
mahogany, mahogany veneer on cherry frame,
tulip; 1760-75; W 58" (147.3 cm); acc. no.
G60.1070.*

Figure 34. *Tea Table. This table has been described as probably of Massachusetts origin.*[11] *The leaf-carved vase of its shaft, fluted pillar, and carving on the edge of its scalloped top relate it to a New York example (Pl. IV), and its paw feet are similar to a New York candlestand (Fig. 26). Without secondary woods and other documentation, however, it can only be stated that this tea table was probably made in New York. Fig. 34: mahogany; 1765–80; H 28⅜" (72.1 cm), Diam 29¾" (75.6 cm); acc. no. G57.513.*

Figure 34

Figure 35   Figure 36

Figures 35, 36, and 37.
*Tea and China Tables.
Within the tenets of
accepted behavior,
practice, and economics
in the Chippendale period
craftsman and patron had a
tremendous opportunity for
choice. These tea tables
provide an excellent
illustration of that fact.
A molded-edge tray (Fig.
35) or a Gothic-arched
pierced gallery (Fig. 36)
prevent tea equipage from
being accidentally swept
from their tops. Another
(Fig. 37), has an
unprotected top like a tea
board supported on a frame.
Its undulating, stepped,
molded edge invites
catastrophe. Carved
gadrooning decorates the
skirts of all the tables,
but one example is of very
high quality (Figs. 37, 37a).*

Figure 36a

Figure 37a

The leaf carving on two examples is similar (Fig. 36a), but on one (Fig. 37a) the carving seems to flow from a branch or twig and ends in fleur-de-lis. Sturdy New York-type claw-and-ball feet support two examples while the third (Figs. 37b, 37c) has a foot that is not square and has well-articulated carved claws (Fig. 5a). The tables are finished on all four sides indicating that they were to be placed away from a wall. Although the type illustrated by Figure 36 is called a "China Table" by Chippendale, he did indicate that they might also be used as tea tables. Fig. 35: mahogany, white pine; 1765-80; H 27¼" (69.2 cm); gift of Lammot du Pont Copeland; acc. no. G53.152.2. Fig. 36: mahogany, white pine; 1765-80; H 28¼" (71.7 cm); acc. no. G52.18. Fig. 37: mahogany, cherry; 1760-80; H 27" (68.6 cm); owned originally by Halstead family of Milton Neck or Rye, N.Y.; acc. no. G59.2840.

Figure 37b

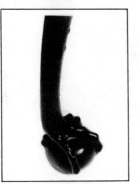

Figure 37

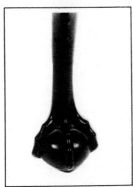

Figure 37c

Figure 38. *Bed. The only stylish feature of this high-post bedstead is fluted decoration on the footposts. Though Philadelphians were generally more style conscious than New Yorkers, there was a market for Queen Anne forms and decoration in Philadelphia throughout the Chippendale period. Poplar was the common wood for bedsteads. In 1777, George Haughton, a Philadelphia upholsterer, advertised for sale "poplar scantling fit for bedsteads."[12] Fig. 38: mahogany; 1755-70; H 96¾" (245.6 cm), L 79¾" (202.6 cm); acc. no. G57.29.* **Figure 39.** *Armchair. Plate XIII (1754 ed.) and Plate X (1762 ed.) of the* Director *provided the design for this fashionable armchair. Related Philadelphia chairs bear the label of James Gillingham (1736-81), but a number of cabinetmakers could have copied the pattern. Rounded or chamfered-edge stump rear legs, pronounced ears terminating the crest rail, S- or reverse-curved armrests ending in scrolled volutes (knuckles), and side rails of the seat tenoned through a mortise in the rear legs (Fig. 51b) are all features of Philadelphia chairs in this period. Fig. 39: mahogany, tulip; 1760-75; H 38¼" (97.1 cm) acc. no. G57.666.*

Figure 39

Figure 40

Figures 40, 41, and 42. *Armchairs. Walnut, a popular cabinet wood of the Queen Anne period, remained in favor in Philadelphia throughout the Chippendale period (Figs. 40, 42). During the English occupation of Philadelphia (1777-78), a storekeeper, William Rush, found that 30 pieces of walnut furniture had been moved into his house by the enemy, including a walnut armchair with blue damask bottom.*[13] *The splat of Figure 40 also occurs on New York and New England chairs, but the stump rear legs, pronounced ears, high-relief carving, reverse S-curve armrests, and shaped*

arm supports are all hallmarks of
Philadelphia furniture shared by these
chairs. Carved rococo shells adorn
the center of the cresting rails of
Figures 41 and 42. The former, a
fashionable mahogany armchair, has
looped arms, a Queen Anne-style
feature of English origin rarely used
by American cabinetmakers.
It is part of a set of chairs (Fig.
65) that were in the Philadelphia
residence of George Washington during
his presidency.[14] Fig. 40: walnut,
arborvitae; 1760-70; H 41½" (105.4
cm); acc. no. G60.1074. Fig. 41:
mahogany, white pine; 1760-85; H
42⅛" (107.3 cm); acc. no. G58.2256.
Fig. 42: walnut; 1760-70; H 40" (101.6
cm); acc. no. G57.531.

Figure 42

Figure 41

Figure 43

Figures 43 and 44. *Armchairs. It is futile to assign a rural or urban origin to furniture solely on the basis of aesthetic criteria.[15] These armchairs, made by William Savery (1721-88), are a case in point. At least one author believes that trifid feet (Fig. 43) were customary on Philadelphia plain chairs throughout the Chippendale period.[16] With the exception of their pierced splats; large, cabochonlike, shaped ears on one (Fig. 43); and beading to outline crest rails, stiles, and armrests these chairs are quite plain. Ironically, because the first example of labeled Philadelphia furniture to be published bore Savery's name, indiscriminate attributions to much*

elaborate Philadelphia furniture were made.
For more than 40 years, however, he
prospered by constructing simple, well-made
furniture (see Fig. 77). Savery made
all sorts of chairs and joiner's work in
his shop, "a little below the Market" in
Second Street. Earlier, the "Sign of
the Chair" hung over its entrance, but
later, that sign was changed to
include a "Chest of Drawers, Coffin,
and Chair." Fig. 43: walnut, yellow
pine; 1755-65; H 40" (101.6 cm);
acc. no. G58.2680. Fig. 44:
mahogany, white cedar, yellow pine,
tulip; 1765-80; H 37¾" (95.8 cm);
acc. no. G60.149.

Figure 44

51

Figure 45

Figure 45. *Armchair. The design of this chair, inspired by Plate XVI of Chippendale's Director (1762 ed.), must have been popular. The chair matches a set of side chairs once owned by John Dickinson, now at Stenton, and is similar to an armchair made for Charles Thomson, secretary of the Continental Congress, as well as a set of side chairs at Winterthur (Fig. 68).*[17] *The best cabinetmakers and carvers in Philadelphia understood that the glory of Chippendale style was ornament. But they also understood the effects of contrast achieved if some surfaces were left plain. This chair's splat was made to appear as an interlaced ribbon. Floral, husk, and leaf carving in high relief decorates its crest rail, stiles, armrests, arm supports, front legs, and knee brackets. Fig. 45: mahogany, white cedar, yellow pine, tulip; 1765-80; H 38¾″ (98.4 cm); no. XIIII in a set; acc. no. G61.116.*

Plate V. *Bed. Late in the Chippendale period,
reeded posts began replacing "fluted pillars" on
bedsteads made in Philadelphia and elsewhere.
In Philadelphia, bedsteads were sold in combinations
ranging in price from a poplar low-post bedstead at
18 shillings to a fluted-and-carved mahogany one at
10 pounds. Adding the cost of European silk taffeta
hangings to an all-mahogany carved-and-reeded bedstead (as in the rare bed illustrated) meant a
significant expense. Pl. V: mahogany; 1780-90; H
95⅛" (241.6 cm), L 90⅝" (230 cm); acc. no.
G55.787.*

Plate V

Plate VI

Plate VI. *Armchair. This armchair is related to another that was presumably made for Governor John Penn (Fig. 48), and the fret carving on its legs also appears on the Marlborough legs of a sofa made by Thomas Affleck (w. 1763-95) for the governor. Here, the rococo leaf-carved knuckles of its armrests, pierced C-scroll leg brackets, and blind frets carved in Gothic and Chinese designs help create a sophisticated chair. European green silk damask (ca. 1725) covers this example. Pl. VI: mahogany, white oak; ca. 1770; H 40" (101.6 cm); acc. no. G56.30.1.*

Plate VII. *Easy Chair. Philadelphia easy chairs are usually upholstered over the seat rails (Pl. VIII). Occasionally, chairmaker, carver, and upholsterer combined to produce the exceptional type shown here (cf. Pl. IX). Its mahogany seat rails and arm supports were left partially uncovered to receive leaf, scroll, and pendant carving; armrest terminals twist outward to provide the unbalanced look of high-style Chippendale-period design. Its upholstery is peach and white French silk (ca. 1725). Pl. VII: mahogany, yellow pine, white oak; 1760-75; H 45″ (114.3 cm); acc. no. G57.665.*

Plate VII

Plate VIII

Plate VIIIa

Plate VIII. *Easy Chair. Horizontal rolled armrests, vertical rolled arm supports—the two forming a C-scroll —upholstered seat rail, and stump rear legs are usual features of Philadelphia easy chairs. Cyma-curved wings return sharply into the armrests in a curvilinear design retained from the Queen Anne style. Carved leaves radiate from a C-scrolled half-cartouche on its knees (Pl. VIIIa). Elegant simplicity, a hallmark of fine Philadelphia craftsmanship, is every-where apparent. The upholstery is Italian red silk damask (1740-60). Easy chairs, frequently used in bed chambers in the 18th century, are now usually placed in living rooms. Pl. VIII: mahogany, yellow pine; 1760-75; H 46⅛″ (117.1 cm); acc. no. G59.1202.*

Figure 46

Figure 47

Figures 46 and 47. *Armchairs. The splat and crest rail of Figure 46 (page 57) is related to other Philadelphia armchairs (Fig. 40). In 1789, Daniel Trotter (w. 1761-80) billed Stephen Girard for a set of six chairs of the type illustrated in Figure 47. The shape of its pierced slats, or splats, has given rise to the term pretzel back for this type of chair. Introduced late in the Chippendale period, it may have been first described in a 1772 Charleston, S.C., advertisement for "carved chairs of the newest fashion, splat Backs, with hollow slats and commode fronts, of the same Pattern as those imported by Peter Manigault, Esq."*[18] *Fig. 46: mahogany; 1760-75; H 39⅞" (101.3 cm); no. III in a set, one of a pair; acc. no. G57.105.1. Fig. 47: mahogany, arborvitae; 1775-90; H 38¼" (97.1 cm); no. I in a set; acc. no. G59.1486.*

Figure 48

Figure 48. *Armchair. Chippendale called armchairs of this type "French chairs with Elbows." This one is said to be part of a set made by Thomas Affleck (w. 1763-95) for Governor John Penn that was bought by Philadelphians at the sale of Penn's furnishings in 1788.*[19] *Similar upholstered armchairs (Pl. VI) are attributed to Affleck. The bead-and-pellet carved molding, an improvement over the design illustrated by Chippendale; relief-carved bellflower and husk in the inset panels of the Marlborough legs; C-scroll brackets; and carved armrest terminals would have cost extra to an initial purchaser. Fig. 48: mahogany; 1760-70; H 42⅛" (107.3 cm); acc. no. G57.668.*

Figure 49

Figure 49. *Armchair. Adapting designs for "French Chairs" in the* Director *(1762 ed.), a Philadelphia chairmaker heeded Chippendale's advice that some styles were "intended to be open below at the Back" to prevent the chairs from appearing heavy. Leaf carving in high relief, of Philadelphia quality, decorates the exposed stiles above the seat. The pronounced ears of the serpentine crest rail bear witness to its Philadelphia origin. Fig. 49: mahogany, red and white oak; 1760-80; H 41⅛" (104.3 cm); acc. no. G61.136.*

Figure 50

Figure 50. *Easy Chair. The tapered rear legs ending
in a platform (a holdover from English style) and the
vertically rolled arm supports are usual on New York
chairs (Fig. 5c; Pl. II). The high-relief carved
C-scrolls, cartouche, husks, acanthus leaves on its
knees and knee brackets, and above all the use of
hairy paw feet place this chair in Philadelphia.
Many Philadelphia upholsterers kept a stock of "easy
chairs in canvas" ready for selection of suitable
fabric.*[20] *Fig. 50: mahogany; 1765-80; H 48½" (123.2
cm); acc. no. 60.1058.*

Figure 51. *Side Chair. Perhaps because this chair was copied from Plate XII (1754 ed.) or Plate XIIII (1762 ed.) of the* Director, *the scroll foot preferred by Chippendale was used. Every detail of the splat and crest rail (Fig. 51a), including carving in very high relief, is employed here. The effect of ornamentation on the front legs and feet is that of architectural carving or wood sculpture. Typically, the side rails of this chair are tenoned through mortises in the rear stump legs (Fig. 51b). Carved gadrooning, used sparingly in Philadelphia, does occur on other chairs and tables (Figs. 53, 64, 96-97, 99-100, 105). Fig. 51: mahogany, white cedar; 1760-80; H 39¾″ (100.9 cm); no III in a set, one of a pair; acc. no. G60.1062.1.*

Figure 51

Figure 51b

Figure 52

Figure 52. *Side Chair: Perusal of a variety of Philadelphia side chairs shows that shaping the lower edges of seat rails relieved the visual problem posed by wide, straight, undecorated rails. The fact that side chairs were usually made in sets is illustrated by the advertisement of George Haughton, a Philadelphia upholsterer, for the sale of "several half dozens of good mahogany chairs."[21] Fig. 52: mahogany; 1760-80; H 40¼" (102.2 cm); no. VIII in a set, one of three; acc. no. G60.1067.1.*

Figure 53

sides of the quatrefoil; provide claw-and-ball feet and Figure 54 emerges. A side chair in the Garvan Collection, Yale University, is identical to Figure 55 and bears the label of Benjamin Randolph (1737/38-39). Differences in carving technique and construction indicate, however, that Figures 53-55 were not made in the same shop. Fig. 53: mahogany, arborvitae; 1765-80; H 38″ (96.5 cm); one of four; acc. no. G60.1066.2. Fig. 54: mahogany; 1760-80; H 38⅛″ (96.8 cm); no. VII in a set, one of four; acc. no. G59.3391. Fig. 55: mahogany, white cedar, white oak; 1760-70; H 37″ (94 cm); no. III in a set; acc. no. G61.1200.1.

Figures 53, 54, and 55. *Side Chairs. Gothic arch and quatrefoil pierced splats were a popular Philadelphia design. The variety possible by playing with a single theme is well illustrated by these chairs. Eliminate carving, pierce the crest rail, use plain Marlborough legs and presto, Figure 55. Substitute hairy-paw feet for the usual claw-and-ball; add carved gadrooning to the front seat rail and to the upper edge of the shoe; partially upholster the seat rail and finish it with brass nails as advocated by Chippendale and Figure 53 is the result. Use C-scrolls and a carved leaf centered on the front seat rail; pierce the splat below and to the*

Figure 54

Figure 55

65

Figure 56

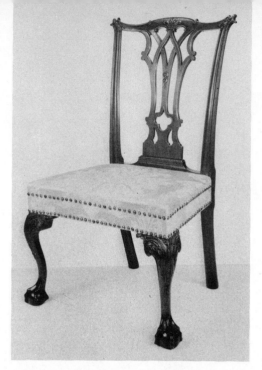

Figures 56, 57, and 58.
*Side Chairs. Chippendale
believed that side chairs
looked best when the
seats were "stuffed over
the rails." A few
Philadelphia chairmakers
followed the London
craftsman's advice (Figs.
56, 71; Pl. IX) even to a
double row of brass nails.
These chairs have legs and
feet associated with
Philadelphia construction,
but their makers drew
freely on Plate X of the
Director (1762 ed.) for
splat, crest rail, and
carving suggestions.
The carved cabochon seen
on much Philadelphia
furniture is on the
pronounced ears of Figure
56. A label (Fig. 58a) of
Thomas Tufft (ca. 1738-88)
appears on Figure 58; but
despite its similarity to
Figure 57—C-scroll-edged
knee blocks, double-arched
skirt edged by C-scrolls,
central foliage carving on
the front rails, and
similar knee carving on
the front legs—it is
unlikely that he made both
chairs. Fig. 56: mahogany;
1765-80; H 38⅛″ (97.1
cm); no. VI in a set; acc.
no. G59.3390. Fig. 57:
mahogany; 1760-80; H
38⅛″ (97.1 cm); acc.
no. 59.3397. Fig. 58:
mahogany, white cedar;
1760-80; H 38⅞″ (98.7
cm); tradition of owner-
ship by Charles Carroll
the Barrister at Mount
Clare, Baltimore, Md.;
no. VI in a set, one of
a pair; acc. no. G57.514.*

Figure 57

Figure 58

Figure 58a

Figure 59

Figure 60   Figure 61

Figures 59, 60, and 61. *Side Chairs. A chair with a back identical to Figure 59 is in the collection of the late Mitchell Taradash. Bearing the label of James Gillingham, it has given rise to the designation of these chairs as Gillingham-type. Many Philadelphia chairs with identical or similar backs survive (Figs. 39, 60). At least 7 different varieties were illustrated by Hornor.*[22] *Given the complex organization of craft activity in Philadelphia, it is unlikely that all were produced in one man's shop. Figures 60 and 61 share pierced corner brackets, beaded-edge seat frames and Marlborough legs, and blind-carved fretwork on stiles and crest rails. Their ears, crest rail shape, and splats are quite different. Philadelphia price lists note that "bases and bragetes [brackets] "could be added to chairs. Evidently the old Philadelphia term for what are now called Marlborough feet was bases. Fig. 59: mahogany; 1765-80; H 39" (99.1 cm); no. I in a set, one of six; acc. no. G61.809.2. Fig. 60: mahogany, white cedar; 1765-80; H 37⅞" (96.2 cm); no. III in a set; acc. no. G61.1198. Fig. 61: mahogany, white cedar; 1765-80; H 38¼" (97.1 cm); no. I in a set; acc. no. G61.1196.*

Figures 62, 63, and 64. *Side Chairs. Strap splat is a modern term often used to describe the interlaced straps and scrolls that formed another type of back for Philadelphia side chairs of this period. New York (Figs. 1, 5-6, 12), Massachusetts, and South Carolina craftsmen had their own interpretations. But with or without a carved tassel at its center, Philadelphia's version is distinct because of the attempt to produce an effect of interlaced wood. Cost usually prevented more effort than is exhibited here, but when not limited*

Figure 62

Figure 63

by economics, Philadelphia's artisans could shape this type of splat to its limit (Figs. 68-69). Much carving on Philadelphia Chippendale period furniture has been termed rococo. No matter how rich and florid the carving (Figs. 62-63), however, it is usually balanced and its elements arranged symmetrically. The asymmetrical leaf carving on the front rails of Figures 62 and 64 is, therefore, exceptional both in quality and design. Outstanding features on these chairs include the carved shell or leaf cap

on the corners of the front seat rail, ears of large carved shells (Fig. 62), and interlaced ribbons of leaf carving on the crest rail (Fig. 63). Fig. 62: mahogany; 1765-80; H 40 1/16" (101.7 cm); no. III in a set; acc. no. G58.2262. Fig. 63: mahogany; 1760-80; H 39 1/2" (100.3 cm); no. III in a set; acc. no. G59.1330. Fig. 64: mahogany; 1760-80; H 39 5/8" (100.6 cm); name PARRISH stamped inside back seat rail; no. I in a set, one of a pair; acc. no. 68.88.1.

Figure 64

Figures 65, 66, and 67. *Side Chairs. Philadelphia chairmakers produced many variations of the pierced strap splat. By eliminating the interlaced effect and adding carving in the "modern" taste, a back such as that of Figure 67 could be produced. Tassel-and-rope carving emphasizes the curved cresting rail of Figure 65 and eliminates the need for a tassel on its splat. Part of a set (Fig. 41), it was among the presidential furnishings of George Washington's residence in Philadelphia.*[23] *Bird-head carving is usually found on armrest terminals of New England or New York chairs (Fig. 1). In Figure 66, a rare variation of the interlaced strap splat, carved bird heads replace the usual volutes, shells, leaves, or cabochon for ears of the crest rail and also replace the usual volutes in the splat. All three examples have fluted stiles and shell carving centered on the cresting and front seat rails. Fig. 65: mahogany; 1765-85; H 41¾″ (106 cm); no. VI in a set, one of two, formerly a set of 5; acc. no. G58.2258. Fig. 66: mahogany, yellow pine, tulip; 1765-80; H 39¾″ (101 cm); acc. no. 53.171.2. Fig. 67: mahogany; 1760-80; H 39¾″ (101 cm); acc. no. G59.1327.*

Figure 65

Figure 66

Figure 67

Figure 68

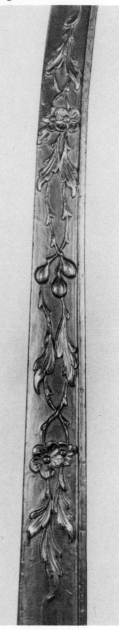

Figures 68 and 69. *Side Chairs. Two of the finest colonial American side chairs, both have their design source in Chippendale's Director (1762 ed., Pls. XVI and IX). Figure 68 is similar to an armchair at Winterthur (Fig. 45) except for the carving on its stiles (Fig. 68a) and legs. It is related to a set of chairs made for John Dickinson, illustrated in Hornor's Blue Book. Figure 69 may be one of a set of chairs made for Thomas Fisher of Wakefield.*[24] *It relies for its success more on an illusion of interlaced wood in its crest rail and splat than on carved, natural ornament. The carved husk on its splat and its knee carving (Fig. 69a) indicate the skills possessed by Philadelphia woodcarvers. In 1770, 6 chairs like Figures 68 or 69 might cost as much as a desk and bookcase. Fig. 68: mahogany, white cedar, yellow pine; 1760-75; H 37¾" (95.9 cm); one of four; acc. no. G52.240.3. Fig. 69: mahogany; 1765-80; H 39" (99 cm); no. VI in a set; acc. no. 56.41.1.*

Figure 69

Figure 69a

Figure 70

Figure 70. *Side Chair. For many years this type of side chair has been attributed to Benjamin Randolph on the basis of labeled examples that are no longer accepted as genuine.*[25] *Hornor illustrates side chairs made by Thomas Affleck that use similar backs and an identical chair is in the Garvan Collection, Yale University Art Gallery.*[26] *All the Philadelphia features are present—carved claw with deep concavities between high-relief knuckles; a ball flattened at top and bottom; stump rear legs; side rails tenoned through rear stiles; and high-relief carving (Fig. 70a). Fig. 70: mahogany, yellow pine; 1765-80; H 39⅛″ (99.3 cm); no. XIIII in a set, one of four; acc. no. G61.803.3.*

Figure 70a

Figures 71 and 72. *Side Chairs. It was noted (Fig.
47) that as early as 1772, Peter Manigault may have
introduced this type of chair to America from
England. In 1783, Martha Washington purchased 24
"Table Chairs," with backs quite similar to Figure
71, as she passed through Philadelphia.*[27] *The name
Peter Kline, branded under the back seat rail of
Figure 71, is probably that of a bricklayer listed
in Philadelphia from 1797 to 1882. Daniel Trotter
(1747-1800) is the Philadelphia cabinetmaker
associated with chairs like Figure 72.*[28] *Fig. 71:
mahogany, hickory, white pine, white oak, tulip,
walnut; 1780-1800; H 37½" (95.7 cm); acc. no.
G59.1487. Fig. 72: mahogany, yellow pine; H 38⅜"
(97.5 cm); acc. no. G57.871.1.*

Figure 73

Figure 73. *Settee. This settee's claw-and-ball feet relate to other Philadelphia seating furniture. Carved shells in high relief on a shaped skirt are also familiar. Carving on the front rail at the juncture of legs and seat was shown on a side chair (Fig. 62). Settees were not a common form of seating furniture in any of the colonies, perhaps because a full-length walnut sofa frame with cabriole legs and carved knees was only slightly more expensive than a settee. Fig. 73: mahogany, white oak, yellow pine; 1765-80; L (seat rail) 66¼″ (168.2 cm); acc. no. G60.1057.*

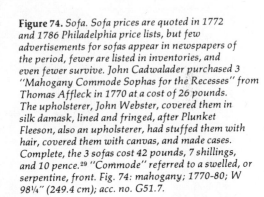

Figure 74. *Sofa. Sofa prices are quoted in 1772 and 1786 Philadelphia price lists, but few advertisements for sofas appear in newspapers of the period, fewer are listed in inventories, and even fewer survive. John Cadwalader purchased 3 "Mahogany Commode Sophas for the Recesses" from Thomas Affleck in 1770 at a cost of 26 pounds. The upholsterer, John Webster, covered them in silk damask, lined and fringed, after Plunket Fleeson, also an upholsterer, had stuffed them with hair, covered them with canvas, and made cases. Complete, the 3 sofas cost 42 pounds, 7 shillings, and 10 pence.[29] "Commode" referred to a swelled, or serpentine, front. Fig. 74: mahogany; 1770-80; W 98¼" (249.4 cm); acc. no. G51.7.*

Figure 74

Figure 75

Figures 75 and 76. *Back-
and Foot Stools. In
discussing a New York
example (Fig. 13) it was
stated that upholstered
side chairs were known in
the Chippendale period as
back stools. Charles
Allen, a Philadelphia
upholsterer, advertised in
1774 that he made "back-
stool chairs."[30] This
form is probably what is
referred to in a Philadelphia
price list of 1772, as
simply "Chair Frame for
Stuffing over back and
Seat with Marlborough feet."
The serpentine front rail
and cyma-curved stiles of
the back frame undoubtedly
were an "extra." A set of*

Figure 76

*back stools at Cliveden,
Germantown, Penn., have
similar backs.[31]
Footstools were rarely made
and few have survived. On
Figure 76, balanced carving
in the "modern taste" on its
knees and brackets combine
with its oval shape as a
reflection of the
classical taste that was
such a strong influence on
English and American
furniture decoration in
the Chippendale period.
Fig. 75: mahogany, red gum,
red and white oak; 1765-80;
H 38⅝" (98.1 cm); acc.
no. G61.1199. Fig. 76:
mahogany; 1755-75; H 17½"
(44.5 cm); acc. no. G56.579.*

Figure 77

Figure 77a

Figure 77. *Chest of Drawers. Without William Savery's label (Fig. 77a), this chest of drawers might have been considered an example of rural cabinetwork. City craftsmen served clients living outside Philadelphia, but there was also a strong demand for plain furniture within the city (Figs. 43, 44). Fluted, chamfered corners, cyma-curve shaped bracket feet, ogee molding on the edges of its top, and quarter-round molding on the drawers are its only decoration. Fig. 77: walnut, white cedar; 1755-65; H 32⅞" (83.5 cm); acc. no. G59.632.*

Figure 78

Figure 79

Figure 78. *Chest of Drawers. A similar chest of drawers at Cliveden,
Germantown, Penn., bears the label of Jonathan Gostelowe (1744-95).*[32]
*Unmarked examples of the same form—fluted, chamfered corners on the case;
canted corner top and front feet to match; ogee bracket feet; and
serpentine front and top—are usually attributed to him. This example was
probably made after 1783 because its original Adam-style drawer pulls and
backplates (Fig. 78a) appear in a catalog of English hardware dating
between 1783 and 1789. Fig. 78: mahogany, yellow pine, tulip; 1780-90;
H 36⅛″ (91.7 cm); acc. no. G59.631.* **Figure 79.** *Chest of Drawers. This
is the usual form of Philadelphia chests of drawers. A case of four long
drawers is supported by swell'd (ogee) bracket feet. Indented quarter
columns, usually fluted, are almost invariably at the front corners. These
bear exceptional relief carving of a floral and leaf vine. Top edges are
usually plain, but these are treated in a very architectural manner with
leaf-and-dart carving. Fig. 79: mahogany, white cedar, yellow pine, tulip;
1760-80; H 35¼″ (89.5 cm); acc. no. G59.1474.*

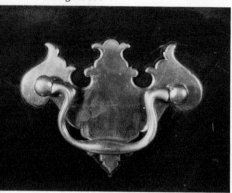

Figure 80. Chest-on-Chest. The top section of a high chest placed on a chest of drawers was known as a chest-on-chest. They were made in all the colonies during the Chippendale period. Charlestonians and New Yorkers preferred theirs with flat tops instead of the broken-arched, scrolled pediments popular elsewhere. Philadelphia examples have 10 to 12 drawers, and price lists indicate that the base charge for this form in mahogany with "scroll pediment, head carved," was 21 pounds. The C-scroll, leaf and tree carving framing a lamb and ewe (Fig. 80a) is balanced but rococo in content and spirit. Indented and fluted quarter columns usually decorate the corners of Philadelphia case pieces. The brasses (Fig. 80b) were still offered in English metal trade catalogs of the late 18th century. The finials and cartouche are replacements made by the late Jesse W. Bair of Hanover, Penn. Fig. 80: mahogany, mahogany veneer, white cedar, white oak; 1760-75; H 86" (218.4 cm); acc. no. G60.1056.

Figure 80a

Figure 81

Figure 81a

Figure 81. *High Chest of Drawers. High chests of drawers were the second most popular type of case furniture made in Philadelphia. Priced 6 pounds less than a chest-on-chest, patrons obtained almost as many drawers, relief from the feeling of weightiness, and the popular cabriole legs and claw-and-ball feet. A carved Chinese and Gothic blind fret decorates the frieze, and large pierced frets tie scrolled arches to a pedestal block at the center of the pediment (Fig. 81a). Handsome relief carving of a large shell, rosette, and ribboned leaves decorates the center drawer of the base section (Fig. 81b). This carving is related in quality and design to that of the famous Van Pelt high chest (Fig. 83). The Delaware River helped to distribute the products of Philadelphia cabinetmakers, as evidenced by the fact that Figure 81 was originally owned by Joseph Shipley of Wilmington, Del. Fig. 81: mahogany, tulip; 1760-75; H 91½" (232.4 cm); cartouche old but replaced; anonymous donor; acc. no. G69.204.*

Figure 81b

Figure 82

Figure 82. *High Chest of Drawers. Was this high chest made early in the Chippendale period, and therefore in Philadelphia, or late in this style period, and therefore in Maryland? Its plain quality does not necessarily make it rural, for much plain furniture was made in Philadelphia. Its wood is walnut, a wood consistently used for Philadelphia furniture during this period. Significantly, a mahogany dressing table of very similar design and decoration was exhibited at The Baltimore Museum of Art in 1968. Evidence for a Maryland origin included "its broad, fluted chamfer and the leaf carving on the knees of the cabriole legs."[33] These are features exhibited by Figure 82, but Philadelphia and New York case furniture often has fluted, chamfered corners. In the absence of fully documented examples, the distinction may never be known. Gerrard Hopkins, a cabinet- and chairmaker from Philadelphia, had a shop on Gay Street, Baltimore, where in 1767 he advertised "Chests of Drawers of various sorts."[34] Fig. 82: walnut, white cedar, tulip; 1755-75; H 96¼" (244.4 cm); acc. no. G59.1862.*

Figure 83

Figure 83. *High Chest of Drawers. Figure 83 and Plate XI are examples of the finest Philadelphia furniture. Added to the basic high-chest form are applied high-relief carving of C-scrolls, rocks, Gothic columns, dripping vegetation, and floral vines (Fig. 83a). Carved leaf ribbons flank a handsome shell and rosette on the center drawer of the lower section (cf. Fig. 81b). On the lower edge of the skirt is a pierced pendant flanked by C-scrolls and leaves. Flowers, husks, and leaves ornament the deeply carved knees of its front legs (Fig. 83b). The typical Philadelphia claw-and-ball foot is evident. Fig. 83: mahogany, white cedar, white oak, yellow pine, tulip; 1765-80; H 90¼" (229.2 cm); cartouche replaced by Jesse W. Bair, Hanover, Penn.; originally owned by John or William Turner and subsequently by the Van Pelt family; acc. no. G58.592.*

Figure 83a

Figure 84

Figure 84. *Desk-on-Frame. Indented, fluted quarter columns, and claw-and-ball feet are the latest exterior features of this desk-on-frame. Used since the late 17th century, only a few were made by the introduction of Chippendale style. The 1772 and 1786 Philadelphia price lists for cabinet-work do not record the form. A serpentine shape, popular in the Chippendale period, was used for a double bank of drawers in the interior of the desk section (Fig. 84a). Fig. 84: walnut, chestnut, tulip; 1755-65; H 42" (106.7 cm); acc. no. G58.2263.*

Figure 84a

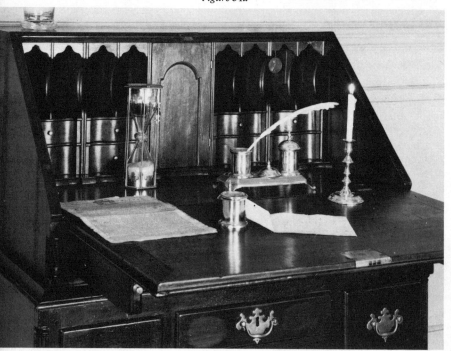

Plate IX

Plate IXb

Plate IX. *Side Chair. This side chair
represents the best type of
Philadelphia chairmaking that has
survived. Described for many years as a
so-called sample chair, it has been
attributed to the Philadelphia cabinetmaker Benjamin Randolph because of its
descent in the family of that
craftsman's second wife. Until 1974,
when 5 side chairs, identical or nearly
so, were sold at Sotheby Parke-Bernet,
this chair was thought to be unique. Not
a sample chair, it could have been made
by a number of excellent Philadelphia
cabinetmakers and carvers. Its
secondary woods; stump rear legs; side
rails tenoned through the rear stiles;
characteristic curved side profile of
its back (Pl. IXa); high-relief
carving of cabochon, leaves, husks
(Pl. IXb); and hairy paw feet mark its
origin as Philadelphia. Its saddle-
shaped seat is unusual, but this
guidebook illustrates other Philadelphia
chairs with partially upholstered seat
rails (Figs. 53, 58; Pl. VII). Although
its carved front seat rail is similar to
the front of a card table made for John
Cadwalader, a chair of this type appears
in a portrait of Lambert Cadwalader
painted by Charles Willson Peale.[35]
Pl. IX: mahogany, arborvitae, white
cedar; 1760-75; H 36⅛″ (93.6 cm);
no. II of a set; upholstered in French
silk lampas, (ca. 1735); acc. no. G58.2290.*

Plate IXa

Plate X

Plate Xa

Plate X. *Sofa. As on Philadelphia chairs, a few of the sofas made there have partially upholstered front rails. Hornor shows a similar sofa, with identical leg carving (Pl. Xa) and partially upholstered seat rail, made in 1783 for George Logan of Stenton by Thomas Tufft (w. 1772-88). George Washington had a similar sofa in his Philadelphia presidential home.*[36] *The name of John Linton (an upholsterer who settled in Philadelphia about 1780) is signed in chalk on the top rail of one of this pair. John Dickinson, "Penman of the American Revolution," was the original owner of these. He lived in Philadelphia until 1794, then moved to Wilmington, Del. The sofas are upholstered in Italian silk damask (ca. 1725). Pl. X: mahogany, white oak, yellow pine; 1775-90; W 79¾" (202.6 cm); one of a pair; acc. no. G58.593.*

Plate XI. *High Chest of Drawers. It is difficult to find carving in the "modern" taste more exuberant and better executed than that used on the high chest and matching dressing table made for Michael and Miriam Gratz in 1769 (Fig. 108, Pl. XIa,). To provide additional variety, the indented quarter columns of its base section are carved but those of the upper section are fluted. Perhaps the largest Philadelphia peanut (cabochon) ever to be carved was placed in the cartouche. The latter appears to be completely asymmetrical in design, like the carved shell at the center of the skirt. The right portion of the cartouche is missing, however, and it was probably balanced by another C-scroll. Michael Gratz's bride was a resident of Lancaster, Penn. It is possible that the abundance of carved decoration on this high chest is a reflection of a design with which she was familiar (cf. Fig. 87). The chinoiserie drawer pulls add another design element of this period to the form. Pl. XI: mahogany, white cedar, tulip; H (cartouche tip) 102½" (260.2 cm); acc. no. G57.506.*

Plate XI

Plate XIa

Plate XII

Figure 85

Plate XII. *Desk and Bookcase. In the Middle Atlantic colonies, maple ranked fourth as a furniture wood.*[37] *Peter Kalm noted that many trees had to be felled to obtain the desirable curled grain.*[38] *Philadelphia chairmakers used maple for rush-bottomed chairs.*[39] *Philadelphia features (Figs. 86-87) include broken arch scrolled pediment with carved rosettes, flame finials, and ogee-bracket feet. Two small drawers, instead of rectangular slides, support the fall-front lid. Pl. XII: maple, white cedar, cherry, tulip; 1760-75; H 95" (241.2 cm); acc. no. 58.1450.* **Figure 85.** *Desk-on-Frame. Marlborough legs and feet; pierced C-scroll brackets between the front rail and legs; and a severe, shaped skirt give Figure 85 an Oriental flavor. Eliminating drawers from the base section and using walnut instead of mahogany lowered its price. Another cost-cutting feature is the one long drawer simulating four small ones flanking the center door. Fig. 85: walnut, tulip; 1760-75; H 43⅝" (110.8 cm); acc. no. G64.1064.*

Figure 86. *Desk and Bookcase. This desk and bookcase is a fine example of the understated elegance frequently presented by Philadelphia Chippendale-style furniture and is also a representative example of its form. Pediments are usually a broken-arch, swan-neck type with carved leaf volutes, as here, or rosettes. On Figure 86, the carved urn of leaves and flowers, carved drapery swag on its pedestal, and pierced fretwork of C-scrolled leaves were undoubtedly "extras." A dentilled cornice is not unusual, and a carved blind fret is often seen on the friezes of Philaldelphia desks and bookcases. Paneled doors sometimes have molded, scalloped edges instead of the rectangular panels shown here. One like this might cost 23 to 26 pounds. Fig. 86: mahogany, white cedar, red gum, yellow pine, tulip; 1760-80; H 100¼" (254.6 cm); acc. no. G56,103.2.*

Figure 86

Figure 87

Figure 87. *Desk and Bookcase. Figure 87 exhibits Philadelphia case furniture techniques. Broken-arch scrolled pediment, carved flame finials, indented quarter columns, and ogee-bracket feet are usual, as are carved rosettes, floral and leaf vines, a tassel (Fig. 87a), and carved pendant on the skirt. Elaborately carved Lancaster County furniture was once thought to be the work of John Bachman II, but recent scholarship has shown that such furniture was made in Lancaster and that the Bachmans produced plain forms. [40] Fig. 87: cherry, tulip; 1785-1800; H 103½" (262.8 cm); originally owned by Michael Withers, near Strasburg, Penn.; acc. no. G51.56.*

Figure 87a

95

Figure 88

Figures 88 and 89. *Fire Screens. There are a few subtle differences, other than carving, that distinguish Philadelphia fire screens from their New York counterparts (Figs. 20, 21). The legs of Philadelphia tripod-base furniture dip closer to a floor surface at the point where the legs end and the feet begin. Urns are more likely to be rounded, and almost a ball, on the shaft of Philadelphia fire screens. The carved claws of Philadelphia tripod-base feet have the high-ridged knuckles that are expected. In this instance (Fig. 88a), the knuckles are scored to imitate a tightly flexed claw. Hairy paw feet (Fig. 89a) are, of course, common only on English or Philadelphia examples.*

A 1772 Philadelphia price list indicates that 2
pounds, 10 shillings was the cost of a mahogany
fire screen with claw feet and leaves on the knees.
Two years earlier, Thomas Affleck billed John
Cadwalader that amount for each of "4 Mahogany fire
screens."[41] At his death in 1776, William Logan had
a mahogany "Fire Skreen," listed with a mahogany
armchair, in the "Back Chamber Northward" of his
Philadelphia town house.[42] Comparison of the turned
poles, shafts, tripod bases, and superlative carving
of these fire screens, reveals minor differences.
Fig. 88: 1765-80; H 60" (152.2 cm); acc. no.
G59.3406. Fig. 89: H 62½" (158.6 cm); acc. no.
G60.1065.

Figure 89

Figure 89a

Figure 90

Figure 90. *Looking Glass. Most looking glasses sold in the colonies were imported. But some locally made examples, including this one in the Chinese taste, have survived (Figs. 90-93; Pl. XIII). Gabriel Valois advertised in 1773 that he made "looking glass frames."*[43] *Often the presence of native American wood is the only means of identifying a Chippendale-style looking glass as American. Fig. 90: gold leaf over white and yellow pine; 1760-85; H 48½" (123.2 cm); one of a pair; acc. no. 58.13.*

Figure 91

Figure 91. *Looking Glass. The Chippendale style remained popular in Philadelphia into the last decade of the 18th century. Figure 91 offers proof of this statement because its makers, James and Henry Reynolds, did not succeed their father until after his death in 1794, and they did not move their shop to Market Street until the following year.*[44] *Their label (Fig. 91a), attached to its original white cedar backboard, noted that they executed and sold carved mahogany looking glasses in "pediment, Mock Pediment, Raffled or Ornamented Frames." A gilt phoenix atop a sawn, scalloped crest; pendant and side ornament in rococo fashion; and indented corners at the top of the glass are Chippendale period features. Fig. 91: mahogany veneer over white pine, white cedar, white pine; 1795-1800; H 49¼"* (125.1 cm); acc. no. G57.535.

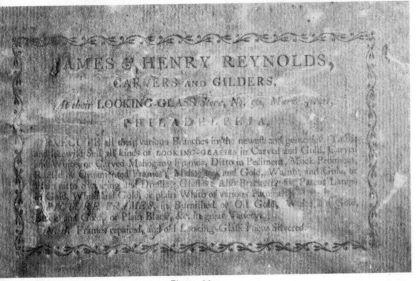

Figure 91a

Figure 92

Figures 92 and 93. *Looking Glasses.
Figure 92 has the label of Joseph White
(Fig. 92a), but it is superimposed over
another label. Some looking glasses
survive that bear both the label of
Joseph White and of the Philadelphia
cabinet- and looking-glass maker, John
Elliott, Sr. (1713-91).*[45]

Figure 92a

Figure 93a

*Significantly, the related looking
glass (Figs. 93, 93a) shown here bears
a partial label of John Elliott, Jr.,
(1739-1810). Fig. 92: mahogany over
white pine, white cedar, tulip; 1760-75;
H 49⅛" (124.6 cm); acc. no. G58.1789.
Fig. 93: mahogany over white pine,
white pine; 1784-1803; H 39⁹/₁₆"
(100.5 cm); acc. no. G58.1776.*

Figure 93

Figure 94

Figure 94. *Looking Glass. Figure 94 reflects several contrasting influences in mid-18th-century Pennsylvania that point to a rural origin. The grafting of Chippendale-period ornaments onto a late William and Mary or early Queen Anne period frame was common practice in northern Europe. Recovered near Lancaster, Penn., this looking glass was probably made in or near that city. Its bold, molded arched frame matches the shape of door panels found on Pennsylvania bookcases (Fig. 87; Pl. XII). Fig. 94: walnut, red or Scots pine; H 60⅛″ (152.6 cm); acc. no. G55.52.*

101

Figure 95. *Candlestand. Except for carving, Figure 95's features are* *Figure 95*
those usually associated with Philadelphia tripod-base stands and tea tables:
a scalloped piecrust top; revolving birdcage with elongated vase-shaped
balusters; fluted pillar; flattened ball turning; a high stance to the legs
with each seeming to touch the floor where its foot begins; and claw feet
with high-ridged knuckles grasping a ball flattened at its top and base.
William Robinson advertised that he made mahogany and walnut stands,[46] *and*
William Logan owned 6 walnut stands at the time of his death.[47] *Fig. 95:*
mahogany; 1760-75; H 28½″ (72.4 cm), Diam 24¼″ (61.6 cm); acc. no. 59.3383.

Figure 96

Figure 96. *Breakfast Table. At the beginning of the Chippendale period, a new form, called a breakfast table, was introduced. It is so described by Chippendale in Plates XXXIII (1754 ed.) or LIII (1762 ed.) of his Director, from which the pierced stretchers and shaped leaves of Figure 96 were adopted. By 1772, breakfast tables were recorded under the general heading of Pembroke tables in the Philadelphia price list for cabinetwork. Drawers in the frame (Figs. 97. 98) were usual, but are lacking in this example. Fig. 96: mahogany, tulip; 1760-80; W (closed) 24⅝″ (62.6 cm), W (open) 48⅛″ (122.2 cm); acc. no. G61.813.*

103

Figure 97

Figure 97a

Figure 97b

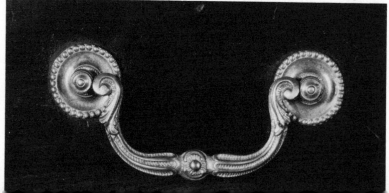

Figure 98

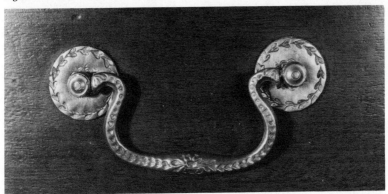

Figure 98a

Figures 97 and 98. *Breakfast Tables. Adam-style brass drawer pulls, tapered spade feet, and the stamp of Adam Hains (Fig. 97a), a Philadelphia cabinetmaker (w. 1788-1803), mark these tables as transitional between Chippendale and Federal period styles. The same shaped top is found on Philadelphia card tables (Figs. 104-105). Figure 97 has no molded edge to its top; uses gadrooning on the skirt instead of pierced brackets; has straight rails and drawer front instead of the commode front of Figure 98, and more delicate saltire stretchers. Fig. 97: mahogany, white cedar, white oak, tulip; 1788-1803; W (open) 40⅜" (102.6 cm); acc. no. G57.669. Fig. 98: mahogany, white cedar, white oak, tulip; 1785-95; W (open) 42" (106.8 cm); acc. no. G59.3401.*

Figure 99

Figure 99. *Card Table. Card tables were as popular in Philadelphia as they were in New York (Figs. 30-32). This shares only one feature with New York tables—a concealed drawer behind the swing leg. Figure 99 has a plain top and rails but richly carved gadrooning on its skirt, C-scroll, husk and leaf carving on knees and brackets (Fig. 99a), and hairy paw feet. This table has been attributed to Thomas Affleck because of its probable ownership by John Cadwalader, but no firm evidence exists to support that conclusion.*[48] *Fig. 99: mahogany, white oak, yellow pine; 1760-80; W 32" (81.2 cm); acc. no. G52.257.*

Figure 99a

Figure 100. *Card Table. Unlike Figure 99 and New York card tables, many Philadelphia examples had a long drawer placed in full view (Figs. 101-103). Plain wood playing surfaces without a cloth cover seem to be the rule for Philadelphia card tables that have survived. The gadrooning applied to the skirt of this table is more subdued than is usually the case with Philadelphia examples. A cartouche surrounded by leaves and C-scrolls is used for knee carving here and on other Philadelphia furniture (Figs. 53, 57-58, 68, 99). Fig. 100: mahogany, tulip; 1765-80; W 33¼" (84.4 cm); acc. no. G59.1338.*

Figure 100

Figure 101

Figure 101. *Card Table.
Card tables with round
corners started at a cost
of 5 pounds for one with
claw feet and plain knees.
With extras, the cost
might go as high as 10
pounds (Fig. 103). Figure
101 bears the label (Fig.
101a) of Benjamin
Randolph (1737/38-91), a
cabinetmaker and skilled
woodcarver, whose trade
card at the Library
Company of Philadelphia
establishes his
reputation as the
Chippendale of colonial
America. Fig. 101:
mahogany, white oak,
tulip; 1765-75; W 33¼"
(84.4 cm); acc. no.
58.85.1.*

Figure 101a

108

Plate XIII

Plate XIII. *Looking Glass. One of the most sophisticated American looking glasses extant, this was made by James Reynolds (1736-94) for John Cadwalader.*[49] *Although perfectly balanced, the carved Gothic pilasters, C-scrolls, ruffles, flowers, rocks, husks, and leaves are combined in the airy spirit associated with rococo taste. This glass is closely related to a group owned by the Fisher and Chew families now at Cliveden.*[50] *Pl. XIII: white and yellow pine, tulip; 1770; H 55½" (141 cm); acc. no. G52.261.*

Plate XIV

Plate XIV. *Side Table. Sideboard tables could be made with either a wooden or marble top. Because of their use for serving beverages and food, marble was preferred. Philadelphia lists for cabinetwork quote prices for both sideboard tables and frames for marble slabs. The latter were slightly more expensive, perhaps because, as Chippendale indicated, frames to support marble tops had to be heavier. Quarries in nearby Chester County, Penn., supplied Philadelphia artisans with gray and white marble (the type used here), but newspapers record that imported marble was also available. The ruffles, curled leaves, and concave cabochon carved on the front rail; shell carving on the round corners; and curved frame with matching top are all evidence of familiarity with contemporary style. Pl. XIV: mahogany and marble; 1760-70; W 52" (132 cm); inner frame, one pair of legs and feet restored; acc. no. G60.1064.*

Plate XV. *Side Chair. This chair may have been part of the furnishings of Mount Clare, built by Charles Carroll the Barrister outside Baltimore.*[51] *A floral and leaf rosette decorates each ear, and leaf carving covers the crest rail. Acanthus leaf and bellflower carving ornaments its broad, interlaced splat. The inner edge of each leg has a broad, tapered chamfer running from seat rail to floor. Southern examples are rare, but the theory that all furniture was imported into the South is being revised as more native examples are found. The seat is covered in cut, uncut, and voided silk velvet (Europe, ca. 1725). Pl. XV: mahogany, beech, white pine, tulip; 1765-80; H 37¹¹/₁₆″ (95.7 cm); one of a pair; acc. no. 61.141.1.*

Plate XV

Plate XVI

Plate XVI. *Side Table. In 1920, this table was bought at an auction in South Carolina and was owned there until acquired by Henry Francis du Pont about 1937. Ever since, a controversy has raged over whether the table was made in Charleston, S.C., or in Philadelphia. An authority on Charleston furniture believes it originated there, and Joseph Downs qualified this provenance.[52] Its secondary wood, yellow pine, was used in both centers. A relationship between craftsmen in both colonies began as early as 1740 when Josiah Claypoole, "From Philadelphia," advertised in the South Carolina Gazette that he made furniture, including "Frames for Marble Tables," warranted for 7 years "the ill usage of Careless Servants only excepted."[53] The quality of this swelled-front table is excellent. Egg-and-dart molding ornaments the top edge of the frame and gadrooning is on its skirt. C-scrolls, leaves, and rosettes appear in cartouche and sunburst patterns on the knees. Pl. XVI: mahogany, yellow pine; 1760-75; W 48″ (121.9 cm); acc. no. G60.1071.*

112

Figure 102. *Card Table. In all examples of card tables with round corners (Figs. 101, 103), the hinged tops follow the shapes of their frames. Here, the upper edge of the rear legs is finished with a half-round molding, a detail that occurs on well-made Philadelphia card tables. A very nice feature of Figure 102 is that the knees of all four legs are carved. Its shaped skirt with volutes is another example of the popularity of Queen Anne design and its use on Chippendale-style furniture in the Quaker City. Fig. 102: mahogany, white cedar, white oak, yellow pine, tulip; 1755-75; W 32⅝" (82.8 cm); one of a pair; acc. no. G58.2247.*

Figure 102

Figure 103

Figure 103a

Figure 103. *Gaming Table. This table, the same type as Figures 101 and 102, is very similar to pairs of card tables in Hornor's Blue Book.* [54] *Carved latticework, C-scrolls, leaves, and ruffles cover the turrets, knees, and rails of this pair of tables (Figs. 103a, b). Should this ornamentation fail to announce the owner's familiarity with the new style, the asymmetrical pendant shell at the center of the skirt would. Fig. 103: mahogany, white cedar, white oak; 1760-75; W (top) 32¼" (81.9 cm); one of a pair; acc. no. G60.1055.1.*

Figure 103b

Figure 104a

Figure 104

Figures 104 and 105. *Card Tables. Wealth, skilled competitors, population growth, and knowledge of fashion were parts of a mixture of ingredients in Philadelphia that produced imaginative variety in furniture design. A straight frame with non-conforming top supported by tapered Marlborough legs provides a contrasting form in Figure 105. Top corners are rounded, like those seen on Philadelphia breakfast tables (Figs. 97-98). A scrolled leaf and cabochon carved shaped skirt (Fig. 104) contrasts with applied gadrooning and pierced C-scroll brackets (Fig. 105). Fig. 104: mahogany, white cedar, white oak; 1765-80; W 34" (86.3 cm); acc. no. G60.1059. Fig. 105: mahogany, white oak, yellow pine, tulip; 1775-85; W 36" (91.4 cm); acc. no. G52.258.*

Figure 105

115

Figure 106. *Card Table. Shortly before the Revolution, the new classical style of the Adam brothers began to affect furniture design. In 1773, in a list of books to be purchased for the Library Company of Philadelphia, was "The Works in Architecture of Robert and James Adam . . . (as far as now Publish'd)."*[55] *This circular card table, with fluted, tapered Marlborough legs, blocklike spade feet, and C-scroll brackets is believed to be the work of Jonathan Gostelowe (w. 1768-93). When Gostelowe advertised in 1793 that he was declining the business of cabinetmaking, his notice included an offer to sell circular card tables.*[56] *Fig. 106: mahogany, white oak, yellow pine, tulip; 1785-93; W 36¼" (92.1 cm); acc. no. 58.46.6.*

Figure 106

Figure 107

Figure 107. *Dressing Table. Popularly called a
lowboy, during the Chippendale period this form was
referred to as a dressing, or chamber, table. At
his death in 1776, William Logan had 6 chamber
tables "with drawers" made of mahogany, walnut, or
maple.*[57] *This table's shaped front skirt, double
arched side skirt, fluted chamfered corners, and
large but subdued shell-carved drawer front are
considered to be features of Maryland Chippendale
furniture.*[58] *But the pages of Hornor's Blue Book
contain illustrations of dressing tables similar to
Figure 107 that were owned by Philadelphia families.
Fig. 107: walnut, tulip; 1760-80; W 34¾" (88.7
cm); acc. no. G53.68.*

Figure 108

Figure 108. *Dressing Table. Figure 108 is the "Table to Suit" the high chest of drawers made in 1769 for Michael and Miriam Gratz of Philadelphia (Pl. XI). Whether of mahogany, walnut, or maple, the form always consists of a long drawer over three smaller ones. Despite the abundance of rich carving—ribboned leaves, ruffles, flowers, cabochon, balanced and asymmetrical shells— enough of its mahogany surface has been left undecorated to provide contrast. Fig. 108: mahogany, white cedar, tulip; 1769; W 37" (94 cm); top is an old replacement; acc. no. G57.505.*

Figure 109

Figure 109. *Bureau Dressing Table.
This form was known throughout the 18th
century as a bureau table, and was most
popular in Philadelphia.*[59] *Price lists
for that city indicate that a mahogany
bureau table with prospect door and
quarter columns (as Fig. 109) cost 8
pounds, 10 shillings. A plain design
for a bureau dressing table, with
3 drawers on each side of a prospect
door, and ogee bracket feet appears
only in the 1754 edition of the
Director. Fig. 109: walnut, yellow
pine; 1755-75; W 39¾" (100.9 cm);
gift of Mr. and Mrs. David Stockwell;
acc. no. G66.138.*

Figure 110

Figure 110. *Dressing or Side Table. It is tempting to relate Figure 110 to furniture made in Lancaster County, Penn. (Figs. 87, 94), but it was probably made in or near Harrisburg, Dauphin County, Penn.*[60] *Its Marlborough legs, relieved by a bead on their outer edges, and "Chinese" brackets are details that help to place it in the Chippendale style. Its bold carved volutes flanking upright and pendant shells, and the cusped arch of its side skirts are vestiges of the Queen Anne period. A dealer acquired this table in 1929 from a descendant of John Harris (d. 1797), a founder of Harrisburg, Penn. Fig. 110: walnut; W 36 1/16" (91.6 cm); acc. no. G58.1928.*

Figure 111. *Side Table. Philadelphia price lists do not quote costs for "side-board tables" or "frames for marble slabs" under 4 feet in width. In his* Director, *however, Thomas Chippendale noted that side tables varied according to the size of rooms. This table must have stood in a small dining room or entry hall. Its weight is relieved by its serpentine curved top and frame, indented corners, and a shaped skirt that is emphasized by carved C-scrolls, leaves, and cabochon. Fig. 111: mahogany, yellow pine, walnut; 1760-75; W 33" (83.8 cm); originally owned by the Smith family, Germantown, Penn.; acc. no. G56.30.2.*

Figure 111

Figure 112. *Side Table. Benjamin
Franklin's Philadelphia home had a pair
of tables "to suit" a sideboard table,
and "marble side boards" were included
in the 1784 sale of the furnishings of
William Hamilton of Bush Hill.*[61] *The
small size of Figure 112 and its mate
might indicate that they were made to
match a larger slab table. The
rectangular shape of its frame,
emphasized by applied gadrooning in the
skirt and balanced shell and leaf
streamers carved on the front rail, was
certainly intended to give an impression
of massive size. Fig. 112: mahogany;
1765-80; W 36" (91.4 cm); one of a pair;
acc. no. G59.3402.*

Figure 112

Figure 113. *China, or Tea, Table. This table should be compared with a New York tray-top china or tea table (Fig. 35). A carved shell is centered on a gadrooned skirt on all sides, indicating that this table was to stand away from a wall. Deep, lush, flower and leaf carving decorates each leg. Philadelphia price lists of 1772 and 1786 refer to this form as a square tea table and indicate that a similar example would cost 6 pounds or more. In 1776, the Philadelphia town house of William Logan contained in the front parlor a mahogany "Tea Table" and a mahogany "China Table."[62] Fig. 113: mahogany, white cedar; 1765-80; W 31¾" (80.6 cm); acc. no. G60.1060.*

Figure 113

Figure 114

Figure 114. *China, or Tea, Table.*
Thomas Chippendale conceived tables
that would hold "a Set of China" or
that "may be used as Tea-Tables." The
serpentine top, rails, and saltire
stretcher of Figure 114 were adapted
from Plates XXXIIII (1754 ed.) or LI
(1762 ed.) of the Director. *Mahogany*
china tables with stretchers and
"commode" or serpentine-shaped tops
are recorded in 1772 and 1786 price
lists in Philadelphia. Such tables
cost more than 7 pounds 10 shillings
without rope-carved edges and bead-and-
reel carved moldings on the legs (as
shown here). Fig. 114: mahogany; 1765-
85; W 32½" (81.9 cm); acc. no. G61.820.

Figure 115

Figure 115. *Tea Table. A cabinetmaker, carver, and turner collaborated to produce this tea table. Hornor noted that cabinetmakers could buy components ready to assemble for tripod-base tables, or send specifications for a particular pillar and top to a woodturner.*[63] *At least one other table like this has survived.*[64] *Elongated baluster or vase-shaped turnings on the birdcage, a flattened ball on the shaft, and typical claw-and-ball feet help to identify this as a Philadelphia table. "A large round mahogany tea table" was included in the inventory of John Cadwalader's house.*[65] *Fig. 115: mahogany; 1765-80; H 28⅛" (71.4 cm), Diam 34 ⅜" (87.3 cm); acc. no. G60.1061.*

Figure 116

Figure 116. *Tea Table. Judging from the number of tables that have survived, card playing and tea drinking were the most popular diversions in colonial America. The shaped top illustrated here (Figs. 116a, 117-118) is the usual form of piecrust edge for circular tea tables and stands. Variation in the decoration of such tables was achieved on this example by extending leaf carving onto the sides of each leg in scroll form; carving the top surface of each leg at its juncture with the shaft; and carving a canopy of gadrooning over the flattened ball of the shaft. Leaf, C-scroll, and ruffle carving (in the "modern" taste on the latter) contrasts with a classical guilloche carved just below it. Fig. 116: mahogany; 1765-80; H 29" (73.7 cm), Diam 29¾" (75.6 cm); acc. no. G58.2215.*

Figure 116a

Figure 117

Figures 117 and 118. *Tea Tables. As with Figure 116, carving extends from the top of the legs of Figure 117 to their sides. Exposed surfaces at the base of the shaft are carved with classical bellflower husks echoing carved decoration of each leg. The flattened ball is undecorated, but the top hides a fluted pillar and a birdcage. A C-scroll cartouche and leaves are carved in a more conventional manner on the legs of Figure 118. Rope carving decorates the upper band of the shaft base, and leaf carving undulates about the surface of the typical flattened ball. Fig. 117: mahogany; 1760-75; H 29⅝" (75.2 cm), Diam 33" (83.8 cm); acc. no. G59.3405. Fig. 118: mahogany; 1760-75; H 28⅞" (73.3 cm), Diam 36⅝" (93 cm); acc. no. G59.3404.*

Figure 118

Figure 119

Figure 119. *Tea Table. Maple furniture is often
given a country origin without hesitation. But maple
was advertised for furniture in Philadelphia.*[66] *This
table exhibits other clues to help assign it a rural
provenance. Carving is rare on country furniture,
and where found doesn't equal the skills of urban
artisans. Here, legs are decorated with stiff,
precise leaves that terminate in a design similar to
the hands of a clock. The block from which the ball
feet were carved is visible. The dished top edge is
shaped to give a stepped effect and the spool, ring,
disc, and vase-shaped turned shaft are evidence of a
skilled, but rural, artisan. It may have been made in
the counties of Delaware, Chester, or Lancaster, Penn.
Fig. 119: maple; 1760-75; H 28½" (72.4 cm), Diam
36¾" (93.4 cm); acc. no. G58.1460.*

Figure 120. *Tall Clock. Relative to other furniture forms, few clocks were produced in colonial America throughout the 18th century. They represented the collaboration of clockmakers for the movements; cabinetmakers or joiners for cases to house the movements; carvers, who ornamented the cases; and merchant importers for the dials, movements, and tools. In 1772, a mahogany case with scroll pediment head, column corners, fret, dentils, shield, roses, and bases cost 12 pounds without glazing and without extra carving. Many features of Philadelphia case furniture are in evidence here, including carved flame-and-urn finials; broken arch pediment with carved rosettes; floral, leaf, and pierced shell carving in high relief; C- and S-scroll blind fret carving; indented, fluted quarter columns; and ogee-bracket feet. Fig. 120: mahogany; 1765-75; H 102⅞″ (261.4 cm); eight-day movement made or assembled by Edward Duffield (1720-1801); acc. no. G52.247.*

Figure 120

Figure 121a

Figure 121

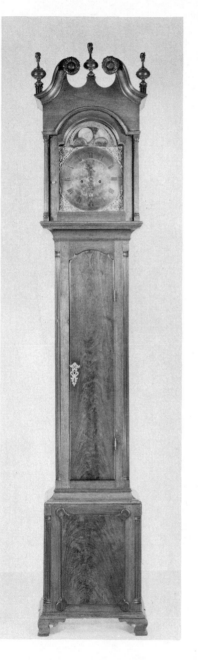

Figure 121. *Tall Clock. It is tempting to correlate the conservative style and plain appearance of Figure 121 with Quaker taste in Philadelphia. Thomas Wagstaffe (1724-1802), the English Quaker craftsman who made its movement, engaged in extensive trade with importers in all of the colonies.[67] His clocks appear in cases ranging from plain to very elaborate. More likely, the customer who ordered this case from William Connell (Fig. 121a) wished to save money. By choosing walnut and eliminating fretwork carving and dentils—but still ordering indented, fluted quarter columns at the corners; carved rosettes, and a scroll pediment head; a raised panel or shield in the base section; and ogee-bracket feet—a customer would pay 8 pounds, thus effecting a saving of 4 pounds. Philadelphia cabinetmakers such as Henry Clifton, John Folwell, and others are known to have produced clockcases.[68] Few bear labels. It is especially frustrating that little is known about William Connell (w. 1760-75) or his work. Fig. 121: walnut, white cedar, yellow pine; 1760-75; H 105" (266.6 cm); eight-day movement; acc. no. G60.1149.*

130

Figure 122

Figure 123

Figures 122 and 123. *Bracket, or Shelf, Clocks. Cases for bracket, or shelf, clocks were also conservative in basic form or shape. Figure 122 has gadrooned molding on its sarcophagus-shaped top; pierced fret-carved spandrels of C- and S-scrolls; hearts and flames; and ogee-bracket feet. All tell a viewer that the owner was conversant with fashionable elements of the new style. The owner of Figure 123 would pay only for leaf and C-scroll blind fret spandrels. By eliminating ogee-bracket feet and other niceties, a considerable sum was saved. Thomas Chippendale refers to these forms as "Table Clock Cases" in his* Director *(1762 ed.). Their name implies that they were displayed on a table rather than on a bracket or shelf. Few American examples have survived. Fig. 122: mahogany, mahogany veneer on yellow pine, tulip; 1771; H 11⅜" (28.8 cm); watch movement by John Morgan, London (w. 1692-1715); assembled by Burrows Dowdney, Philadelphia (advertised 1768-71); acc. no. G61.516. Fig. 123: mahogany; 1765—90; H 18⅛" (46 cm); eight-day movement by Robert or Thomas Best, London (w. 1765-94); assembled by Edward Duffield, Philadelphia (1720-1801); acc. no. G58.1929.*

Figure 124

Figure 124. *Tall Clock.* Philadelphia cabinetwork
influenced woodworkers in Delaware, Maryland, New
Jersey, and rural Pennsylvania. This clockcase
was probably made in or near Reading, Berks County,
Penn. Chamfered corners on the base section;
indented, fluted quarter columns on the
pendulum case; a carved shell above a shaped door
in the same section (Fig. 124a); and scroll pediment
with carved rosettes are hallmarks of Philadelphia
clockcases. While it is conceivable that this case
was made in Philadelphia and shipped to Reading,
the execution of its carving speaks of a rural
provenance. The design and carving of this clockcase are not closely related to Lancaster County
examples.[69] Its bracket feet are more like the
designs of George Hepplewhite and Thomas Sheraton,
and its enameled dial is a type imported in large
quantities following the end of the American
Revolution. Fig. 124: walnut, white pine; 1785-
1800; H 100¾″ (255.8 cm); eight-day movement;
assembled and made by Daniel Rose (1749-1827),
Reading, Penn.; acc. no. 65.2.

Figure 124a

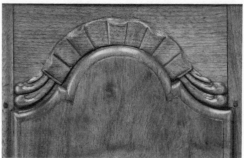

Figure 125

Figure 125. *Tall.Clock. Thomas Crow (w. 1770-1824), a Wilmington clockmaker, whose name appears on this dial, advertised at least once in the* Pennsylvania Gazette *and was familiar with craft activity in Philadelphia.*[70] *The C-scrolls, flowers, and leaves applied to the pediment are among the best examples of Philadelphia carving. So, too, are the carved rosettes and rococo cartouche with leaf-carved cabochon at its center (Fig. 125a). Like Figure 120, this case would have been expensive. Fig. 125: mahogany; 1770-80; H 102⅛″ (259.2 cm); movement assembled or made by Thomas Crow; acc. no. G64.968.*

Figure 126a

Figure 126b

Figure 126

Figure 126. *Tall Clock. Another labeled clockcase (Fig. 126a) gives evidence of the influence of Philadelphia's version of the Chippendale style outside its environs and of the retention of that style quite late in the 18th century. Ogee bracket feet, indented fluted quarter columns at the corners of the base and pendulum case sections, a cyma-curved raised panel or shield, and scrolled pediment atop a straight cornice (Fig. 126b) are features of Philadelphia clockcases. But from the convenient date supplied by the Cantwell's Bridge casemaker, it is clear that it was made in 1795. More than 20 years earlier, John Janvier, Sr. (1749-1801) had advertised that he was from Philadelphia when he set up shop in Elkton, Md. Fig. 126: walnut, white cedar, tulip; 1795; H 94¾" (240.6 cm); finial not original; acc. no. 64.175.*

Figure 127   **The South**

Figure 127. *Armchair. The clear identification of Southern-made furniture is not always possible (Pl. XVI). Maryland was influenced both by furniture and craftsmen from Philadelphia. "Bold appearance, exaggerated ears, heavy carving, broader splat, lacking delicacy of proportion," are phrases used to describe furniture that bears Philadelphia features but is different in overall appearance. Secondary woods are the same in both Maryland and Pennsylvania, so it is best to indicate that chairs like this were made in either place. Fig. 127: mahogany, tulip; 1765-80; H 41⅜" (105.1 cm); acc. no. G57.504.*

Figure 128

Figure 128. *Armchair. Philadelphia influence is discernible, but the heavy C-scrolled arm supports are not like the reverse cabriole leg seen on most Philadelphia armchairs. The pierced strapwork splat is also much wider than usual. The ruffle on the crest rail, leaf at the center of the splat, shell on the front seat rail, and leaves on the front legs are all evidence of a skilled Maryland (probably Baltimore) carver. Fig. 128: mahogany, arborvitae; 1755-65; H 39⅝″ (100.6 cm); acc. no. G57.667.*

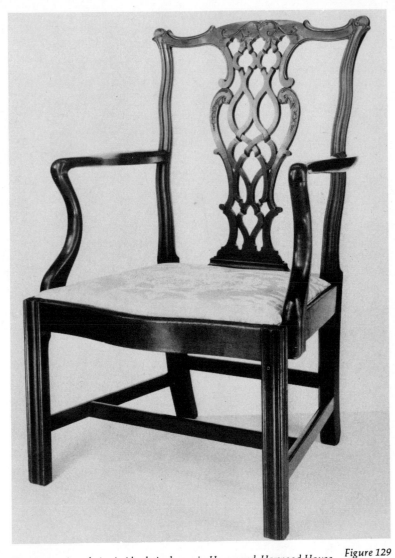

Figure 129

Figure 129. *Armchair. A side chair shown in Hammond-Harwood House is identical in its splat design, carving, stiles, and molded front Marlborough legs.*[71] *The serpentine-shaped front seat rail, concave arm supports, reverse S-curved armrests, and curving stiles give a visual impression of movement and restlessness that would have pleased any exponent of the "modern" taste. Fig. 129: mahogany, yellow pine; 1765-80; H 39⅛" (99.3 cm); acc. no. G51.24.*

Figure 130

Figure 130. *Easy Chair. At least 3 Southern easy chairs have survived that share the vertically scrolled arm supports and armrests; broad surfaced knees on the front legs; tapered rear legs ending in a pad or platform; and New York- or Massachusetts-type claw-and-talon grasping a ball exhibited by this chair.*[72] *Figure 50, a Philadelphia chair, has similar features. Undecorated surfaces in this period indicate conscious choice rather than lack of sophistication or skill. In 1771, Peter Manigault wrote to his London agent to send furniture and silver "the plainer the better so that they are fashionable."*[73] *Fig. 130: walnut; 1750-70; H 44" (111.8 cm); tradition of ownership by the Lewis family of Virginia; acc. no. 51.72.1.*

Figure 131

Figure 131. *Side Chair. This chair shares the wide splat, ogee molded front Marlborough legs, and exaggerated ears often ascribed to Maryland chairs (Figs. 127-29; Pl. XV). The design of the splat owes more to Robert Manwaring's The Cabinet and Chairmaker's Real Friend and Companion (London, 1765) than it does to Chippendale's Director. Such designs were frequently adapted by Massachusetts craftsmen, and it may be significant that the lower portion of the rear legs is raked backward, a practice followed by Bay State chairmakers. As early as 1747, an importer in Annapolis offered maple desks and chairs from New England to his customers.[74] Fig. 131: mahogany; 1765-80; H 37½″ (95.2 cm); acc. no. 51.64.7.*

Figure 132. *Chest of Drawers. In recent years, much fine furniture has been identified as the product of cabinetmakers working in the Shenandoah Valley of Virginia and Piedmont areas of North Carolina and Georgia. Figure 132—with strings of inlay on its drawer fronts forming a panel with incurved corners; inlaid heart-shaped medallions; string inlay instead of fluting running the length of indented quarter columns at the corners (Fig. 132a); bold, large, ogee-bracket feet; and a vertical bead finishing the rear edges of its sides—resembles case furniture made in the Catawba area of the North Carolina Piedmont.[75] Heart-shaped motifs were not confined to the Pennsylvania Germans: they are found on furniture made by Anglo-American craftsmen who worked in Connecticut, New York, and Pennsylvania (Fig. 122). Fig. 132: walnut, white oak, yellow pine; 1780–1810; H 65 1/16" (165.3 cm); acc. no. G67.1724.*

Figure 132

Figure 132a

Figure 133. *Candlestand. This stand was purchased in Craven County, N.C., and some believe it is of Southern origin, probably Charleston, S.C.[76] The stance of its tripod-base legs seem Philadelphia-inspired, but its oversized claw feet; fully delineated ball; and baluster, or vase-shaped, pillar just under the birdcage section are unrelated to Northern-made stands and its carving doesn't have the lush quality associated with Philadelphia. Fig. 133: mahogany; 1765-80; H 27⁷/₁₆" (69.7 cm), Diam 25⅝" (65.1 cm); acc. no. G52.259.*

Figure 133

Figures 134 and 135. *Kettle, or Urn, Stand and China, or Tea, Table. The unusual foot on this kettle stand (Fig. 134) appears on a Southern marble-top side table with a blind-fret carved frieze on its frame.*[77] *Figure 135 is described in Philadelphia price lists as a china table "three feet long, Bases [Marlborough] feet and Brackets with fret Frame." Such a mahogany table cost 8 pounds in Philadelphia, but Thomas Elfe charged 20 pounds for a "China frett tea table" in Charleston, S.C.*[78] *Inflated currency probably accounts for the disparity in price. Fig. 134: mahogany, tulip; 1765-80; H 25⅜" (64.5 cm); probably Charleston, S.C.; acc. no. G52.63. Fig. 135: mahogany, white pine, tulip; 1765-80; H 25⅞" (65.7 cm); probably Charleston, S.C.; acc. no. G52.141.*

Figure 134

Figure 135

Notes to the Illustrations

1. Homer Eaton Keyes, "A Clue to New York Furniture," *Antiques* (March 1932), pp. 122-23.
2. Advertisement inside front cover, *Antiques* (July 1946). "Museum Accessions," *Antiques* (March 1971). Helen Comstock, *American Furniture: Seventeenth, Eighteenth, and Nineteenth Century Styles* (New York: The Viking Press, 1962), no. 302.
3. Norman S. Rice, *New York Furniture Before 1840 in the Collection of the Albany Institute of History and Art* (Albany, N.Y.: Albany Institute, 1962), pp. 18, 26-27.
4. *The New-York Gazette*, July 12, 1762.
5. Rita S. Gottesman, *Arts and Crafts in New York, 1726–1776* (New York: New-York Historical Society, 1938), pp. 110, 134.
6. *The New-York Gazette*, Jan. 27, 1763, as quoted in Gottesman, p. 124.
7. Rice, p. 18.
8. Joseph Downs, *American Furniture: Queen Anne and Chippendale Periods* (New York: Macmillan, 1952; reissued by The Viking Press, New York, 1967), no. 277.
9. Morrison H. Heckscher, "The New York Serpentine Card Table," *Antiques* (May 1973), pp. 974-83.
10. As quoted in Gottesman, p. 125. As quoted in Downs, no. 358.
11. Downs, no. 383.
12. *Pennsylvania Journal*, March 12, 1777.
13. Alfred Coxe Prime, *The Arts & Crafts in Philadelphia, Maryland, and South Carolina, 1721–1785* (Topsfield, Mass.: The Walpole Society, 1929), p. 191.
14. Stephen Decatur, "George Washington and his Presidential Furniture," *American Collector* (Feb. 1941), pp. 8-11, 15.
15. Nancy Goyne Evans, "Unsophisticated Furniture Made and Used in Philadelphia and Environs," *Country Cabinetwork and Simple City Furniture* (Charlottesville, Va.: The University Press of Virginia, 1970), pp. 151-203.
16. John T. Kirk, *American Chairs: Queen Anne and Chippendale* (New York: Alfred A. Knopf, 1972), pp. 6-7.
17. William Macpherson Hornor, Jr., *Blue Book, Philadelphia Furniture, William Penn to George Washington* (Philadelphia: privately printed, 1935), pls. 119, 225, 341.
18. Prime, p. 176.
19. Hornor, p. 184, pl. 259.
20. Prime, p. 207.
21. Prime, p. 171.
22. Hornor, pls. 342-49.
23. Decatur, pp. 8-11, 15.
24. Hornor, pls. 113-15, 119, pp. 204-5.
25. Edwin J. Hipkiss, *Eighteenth-Century American Arts: The M. & M. Karolik Collection* (Cambridge, Mass.: Museum of Fine Arts, Boston, 1941), no. 89, p. 152. Kirk, nos. 81, 83, pp. 86-87, 172-74.
26. Hornor, pls. 260, 265.
27. Hornor, pp. 222-24, pls. 289, 365-72. Charles F. Montgomery, *American Furniture, The Federal Period* (New York: The Viking Press, 1966), nos. 81-82.
28. Milo M. Naeve, "Daniel Trotter and his Ladderback Chairs," *Antiques* (Nov. 1959), pp. 442-45.
29. Nicholas B. Wainwright, *Colonial Grandeur in Philadelphia* (Philadelphia: Historical Society of Pennsylvania, 1964), pp. 41-42, 44, 51.
30. Prime, p. 200.
31. Hornor, pl. 262.
32. Hornor, pl. 107.
33. William Voss Elder, II, *Maryland Queen Anne and Chippendale Furniture of the Eighteenth Century* (Baltimore: The Baltimore Museum of Art, 1968), no. 50, pp. 72-73.
34. Downs, no. 199.
35. Wainwright, pp. 114-19.
36. Hornor, pls. 99, 231.
37. Prime, pp. 172, 184.
38. Downs, no. 233.
39. Evans, p. 166.
40. John J. Snyder, Jr., "The Bachman Attributions: A Reconsideration," *Antiques* (May 1974), pp. 1056-65.
41. Wainwright, p. 44.
42. Frederick B. Tolles, "Town House and Country House," *The Pennsylvania Magazine of History and Biography* (Oct. 1958), pp. 397-410.
43. Prime, pp. 225-26.
44. Alfred Coxe Prime, *The Arts & Crafts in Philadelphia, Maryland, and South Carolina, 1786–1800 Second Series* (Topsfield, Mass.: The Walpole Society, 1932), p. 234.
45. Prime, p. 196.
46. Prime, p. 180.
47. Tolles, pp. 403-4.
48. Wainwright, p. 120.
49. Wainwright, pp. 46, 124-25.
50. Hornor, pls. 228, 438, 439.
51. Elder, no. 12.
52. E. Milby Burton, *Charleston Furniture, 1700–1825* (Charleston, S.C.: The Charleston Museum, 1955), fig. 94, p. 50. Downs, no. 361.
53. Prime, p. 163.

54. Hornor, pls. 234-35.
55. A Book of Minutes belonging to the Director of the Library Company of Philadelphia. Library Company of Philadelphia MS II, p. 97.
56. Montgomery, no. 285.
57. Tolles, pp. 403-4.
58. Elder, nos. 49-50.
59. Nancy Goyne Evans, "The Bureau Table in America," *Winterthur Portfolio 3* (Charlottesville, Va.: The University Press of Virginia, 1967) pp. 24-36.
60. Articles on Lancaster County furniture by John Snyder, Jr., appear in *Antiques* (May 1974 and May 1975).
61. Hornor, pp. 135-36. Prime, p. 193.
62. Tolles, p. 401.
63. Hornor, pp. 142-43.
64. Hornor, pl. 230. *Antiques* (April 1968), p. 487. *Antiques* (Oct. 1975), inside front cover.
65. Wainwright, p. 73.
66. Prime, pp. 172, 184, 186.
67. Martha Gandy Fales, "Thomas Wagstaffe, London Quaker Clockmaker," *The Connoisseur* (Nov. 1962), pp. 193-201, fig. 10.
68. Hornor, pp. 126-27.
69. Snyder (May 1974).
70. Prime, pp. 236-37.
71. Elder, no. 10.
72. Paul H. Burroughs, *Southern Antiques* (Richmond, Va.: Garret & Massie, 1931), pl. 14, p. 163. Helen Comstock, "Southern Furniture Since 1952,"*Antiques* (Jan. 1967), fig. 15, p. 108. Virginia Museum of Fine Arts, *Southern Furniture, 1640–1820* (New York: Antiques, 1952), no. 62.
73. Comstock, "Southern Furniture," p. 102.
74. Prime, p. 187.
75. Frank L. Horton, "The Museum of Early Southern Decorative Arts," *Antiques* (Jan. 1967), p. 85. Virginia Museum of Fine Arts, nos. 72, 109, pp. 35, 46.
76. The Valentine Museum, *Charles Navis: Tastemaker* (Richmond, Va.: 1967), fig. C, p. 13. Downs, no. 287.
77. Virginia Museum of Fine Arts, no. 155, p. 61.
78. Burton, p. 50.

Suggested Reading

Burton, E. Milby. *Charleston Furniture, 1700-1825.* Charleston, S.C.: The Charleston Museum, 1955.

Chippendale, Thomas. *The Gentleman & Cabinet-Maker's Director.* New York: Dover Publications, Inc., 1966. Reprint of 1762 edition.

Comstock, Helen. *American Furniture: Seventeenth, Eighteenth, and Nineteenth Century Styles.* New York: The Viking Press, 1962.

————. "Southern Furniture Since 1952," *Antiques* (Jan. 1967), pp. 102-19.

Downs, Joseph. *American Furniture: Queen Anne and Chippendale Periods.* New York: Macmillan, 1952. Reissued by The Viking Press, 1967.

Elder, William Voss, II. *Maryland Queen Anne and Chippendale Furniture of the Eighteenth Century.* Baltimore: The Baltimore Museum of Art, 1968.

Hipkiss, Edwin J. *Eighteenth-Century American Arts. The M. & M. Karolik Collection.* Cambridge, Mass.: Museum of Fine Arts, Boston, 1941.

Hornor, William Macpherson, Jr. *Blue Book, Philadelphia Furniture, William Penn to George Washington.* Philadelphia: Privately printed, 1935.

Horton, Frank L. "The Museum of Early Southern Decorative Arts. The Rooms and Their Furnishings," *Antiques* (Jan. 1967), pp. 72-95.

Ince, William and Mayhew, John. *The Universal System of Household Furniture.* Chicago, Ill.: Quadrangle Books, 1960. Reprint of 1762 edition.

Kimball, S. Fiske. *The Creation of the Rococo.* Philadelphia: Philadelphia Museum of Art, 1943.

Kirk, John T. *American Chairs: Queen Anne and Chippendale.* New York: Alfred A. Knopf, 1972.

————. *Early American Furniture.* New York: Alfred A. Knopf, 1970.

Manwaring, Robert. *The Cabinet and Chairmaker's Real Friend and Companion.* London: John Tiranti, Ltd., 1954. Reprint of the 1765 edition.

Miller, V. Isabelle. *Furniture by New York Cabinetmakers, 1650-1860.* New York: Museum of the City of New York, 1957.

Randall, Richard H., Jr. *American Furniture in the Museum of Fine Arts, Boston.* Boston: Museum of Fine Arts, 1965.

Rice, Norman S. *New York Furniture Before 1840 in the Collection of the Albany Institute of History and Art.* Albany: Albany Institute, 1962.

Sack, Albert. *Fine Points of Furniture: Early American.* New York: Crown Publishers, Inc., 1950.

Schiffer, Margaret B. *Furniture and Its Makers of Chester County, Pennsylvania.* West Chester, Pa.: Chester County Historical Society, 1966.

Stitt, Susan. *Museum of Early Southern Decorative Arts.* Winston-Salem, N.C.: Old Salem, Inc., 1970.

Theus, Mrs. Charlton M. *Savannah Furniture, 1735-1825.* Savannah, Ga.: Privately printed, 1967.

Virginia Museum of Fine Arts. *Southern Furniture, 1640-1820.* New York: Antiques, 1952.

Wainwright, Nicholas B. *Colonial Grandeur in Philadelphia. The House and Furniture of General John Cadwalader.* Philadelphia: Historical Society of Pennsylvania, 1964.

Warren, David B. *Bayou Bend. American Furniture, Paintings and Silver from the Bayou Bend Collection.* Houston, Texas: The Museum of Fine Arts, 1975.